SECOND THOUGHTS
FOR SKEPTICS

SECOND THOUGHTS
FOR SKEPTICS

DOUGLAS D. WEBSTER

REGENT COLLEGE PUBLISHING
Vancouver , British Columbia

Regent College Publishing
5800 University Blvd.
Vancouver, BC V6T 2E4 Canada
www.regentpublishing.com

The author and publisher wish to thank
Jim Meals and Jason Fincher for their editorial assistance.

Library and Archives Canada Cataloguing in Publication

Webster, Douglas D.
Second thoughts for skeptics / Douglas D. Webster.

Includes bibliographical references.
ISBN 978-1-57383-450-6

1. Apologetics. 2. Spirituality. I. Title.

BT1103.W44 2010   239   C2010-902713-2

for Andrew and Jeanine

CONTENTS

INTRODUCTION

On my way home from work one day I listened to Julia Sweeney's story, "Letting Go of God," on National Public Radio's *This American Life*. Her youthful tone of innocence and her spirited story-telling kept me listening—she didn't sound like she had an axe to grind. A more serious and combative atheist arguing against Christianity would have turned me off, but I was hooked on Julia's amusing journey into unbelief. In just twenty-nine minutes and without uttering a harsh word, she attempted to shred the credibility of the Bible from Genesis to Revelation.

I assume NPR broadcasts a one-woman monologue like Julia Sweeney's without rebuttal because it is classified as "entertainment." Equal air-time applies to Democrats and Republicans. It does not extend to disputing biblical truth claims. "Letting Go of God" was never meant to be a serious piece anyway, but only a clever and artsy human interest story. That's the subtlety of the situation, because Julia's monologue is a serious and disarming criticism of the Christian Faith. Under the cover of a human interest story, Julia Sweeney has waged her sweet attack against the Bible with innuendo, false associations, and misleading impressions.

Julia begins her story with a visit by two Mormon missionaries who came to her door with a message from God. Before she knew it, these two Mormon "boys" launched into the story of Mormonism, beginning with Leehigh's visit to America from Jerusalem in 600 BC. She found the whole thing (Joseph Smith, the gold plates, the heavenly family) all utterly incredible and silly, but then she realized that the only reason she found Roman Catholic theology credible was because she was used to it. Who could honestly believe that God impregnated a virgin (with a baby who turned out to be the Son of God)? Her conclusion: Mormonism and Roman Catholic dogma are equally ridiculous.

Nevertheless, this encounter inspired Julia to explore her faith. She was raised Roman Catholic and had found it to be a great experience, but she had never really studied the Bible. So, she started attending a Bible study in her local parish, but the more she read the Bible, the more disillusioned she became. She found the Bible contradicting itself all over the place. She found contradictions in the first two chapters of Genesis. She thought people who claim the Bible is true must not have read the first two chapters. She was shocked by God's judgment in the days of Noah and appalled by the sordid tale of Lot and his daughters. "I knew the Bible had nutty stories," she said, "but I guess I thought they would be wedged in amidst an ocean of inspiration and history, but instead the stories just got darker and more convoluted, like when God asked Abraham to murder his son Isaac. As a kid we were taught to admire it. I caught my breath reading it. Admire it! What kind of sadistic test of

INTRODUCTION

loyalty is that to ask someone to kill his or her child? And isn't
the proper answer, 'No, I will not kill my child or any child'?"

For Julia, the Bible is filled with creepy sacrifice-your-off-
spring-stories, archaic hard to imagine laws, and unbelievable
conclusions. She is certain that the Book of Revelation is the
most odd-ball book of the Bible because it claims only 144,000
people will get into heaven. Never mind that John is using
numbers symbolically and writing in a literary genre that needs
to be appreciated in order to understand what he's saying.
The Bible is up for ridicule, not interpretation. Julia leaves the
impression that it is only an odd assortment of shocking stories
that are both offensive and nonsensical. She flits through the
Bible with an attitude that if it's in the Bible, the Bible must
endorse it. Thus she claims the Bible condones rape, polygamy,
child-sacrifice, and other atrocities. Her conclusion: "Some
people argue that without the Bible, morality would be relative
and wishy-washy, but in the Bible morality is relative and
wishy-washy. In fact, it sure seems like our modern morality is
much more loving and humane than the Bible's morality."

Jesus only adds to her disappointment. She finds him much
angrier than she imagined. She claims it is hard to stay on Jesus'
side when he says hateful, aggressive things. It is "downright
crazy" when he curses the fig tree just because it doesn't
have figs. But the most upsetting thing about Jesus for Julia is
his family values. He seems to have no ties to family and he
discourages his converts from having any contact with their
families. She accuses Jesus of doing the same thing the cults
do when they try to separate you from your family so they
can inculcate you into their crazy cult. Everything she says is
cynical to the core, but said in such a sweet and innocent way
that her audience is bound to take her word for it. When she

says, "The Bible, the good book, the good news, the gospel," her tone is pure mockery. The whole thing makes her want to ask Bible-toting church goers if they had ever bothered to read the Bible, because, as she says, "if you cared enough to look inside you would find that you opened the door to an insane asylum, with a bunch of crazy people walking around inside."

But in the end, it is not just the sordid tales and crazy stories that bother Julia, but the whole point of the New Testament— that Jesus came to die for our sins, "as if someone can suffer for our sins." From Julia's perspective, what's the big deal about Jesus' suffering? By comparison, Julia's brother, who died from cancer suffered a whole lot more than Jesus did. "So, okay Jesus suffered," she says in a condescending tone. "I mean Jesus apparently suffered terribly for one maybe even two days. I heard someone say once that Jesus had a really bad weekend for our sins." For Julia Sweeney the whole thing is absurd. "Why would a god create people so imperfect, blame them for their own imperfections, and then send his son to be murdered by those imperfect people to make up for how imperfect those people were and how imperfect they were inevitably going to be. I mean, what a crazy idea."

Having reached the conclusion that all she could appreciate about the church was the stained glass windows, the religious art, the songs (but not the words, only the melodies), it wasn't very long before Julia realized that there was a tiny little thought that whispered, "There is no God." As she says, over the course of several weeks, God disappeared altogether. She had, in her words, "let go of God." She realized that life is random. It is what it is. Her thoughts are, and always will be, completely her own. There is no justice and nothing happens to us after we die. We just die.

I finished listening to her story and I wondered what C. S. Lewis would say to Julia. How would the great twentieth century convert from atheism to Christianity respond to an entertaining skeptic who had let go of God with such clever confidence? What might cause her to rethink her conclusions? Would a thoughtful response have an effect on her? In the 60's believers contended with tightly reasoned disbelief, but today, we are entertained by personal stories of disillusionment. Instead of a fully armored, reasoned assault on the truth, a fashion-conscious skeptic like Julia is conveniently dressed in subjective attitudes and first impressions. Flippancy, sarcasm, irony, and humor are the preferred weapons of unbelief. In the court of public opinion, today's skeptic is looking for a quick dismissal of the Bible, not some long, dragged out, serious discussion of the truth. With a well-timed joke or an amusing anecdote, she hopes this whole business of Christ and the Bible can be "laughed out of court."

Christians should not be surprised that the new forum for such matters is entertainment. Discussing the Bible has been off limits in the public school classroom for allegedly violating the laws of the land, and out-of-place in the university for being unworthy of intellectual consideration. That leaves few places outside of the church and the home where the Bible can be discussed seriously. And even in these places, the culture of entertainment is so pervasive that serious discussion about the truth is nearly impossible. Television substitutes for the forum of the family meal and churches feel the pressure to entertain. Neil Postman warned that this is what would happen in the age of entertainment. Before too long we would have amused ourselves to death. Christians, by virtue of their commitment and devotion to Christ, seem ill-prepared to excel in the field of entertainment. Besides, the Bible doesn't work well in light-hearted discourse. It is like trying to tell God's great salvation history story on the David Letterman Show. But Julia Sweeney could tell her story on the Lettermen show and the audience would love it.

I would like to have an in-depth conversation with Julia about the Gospel, not to debate her, but to reason with her. Our purpose might be to take a fresh look at what she finds so contradictory and crazy in the Bible. I'm not sure the conversation would change either of us, but she might see the Bible in a different light. She might. But we can't do this kind of work over sound bites and anecdotes. We have to apply our minds and hearts to this kind of work. Julia has concluded that life is random and death ends all—that's one hell of a conclusion. So this work is going to take time, a lot longer than twenty-nine minutes, but what better way to spend our time? We have nothing to lose and everything to gain.

1

MEANINGLESS! MEANINGLESS!

"Meaningless! Meaningless!" says the Teacher. "Utterly meaningless! Everything is meaningless."

Ecclesiastes 1:2 NIV

The question of meaning is not only an unavoidable existential question but a basic scientific question. Truth unites what the modern academic experience divides. We can neither live well nor do science well without meaning. Theological reflection is both devotional and scientific. It is devotional when it deepens our devotion to God, and it is scientific when it deepens our understanding of God's creation. In fifth grade, my son memorized a dictionary definition of science: "Science is the observation, identification, description, experimental investigation, and theoretical explanation of phenomena." This fits theology well, because both theology and science are revelatory—both begin with God. Nature alone—life extracted from God—is only a figment of the modern imagination. The basic myth that postulates meaninglessness in order to do science is an irrational contradiction that deserves to be

15

exposed as a modern heresy.

Situation comedies, such as *Seinfeld* or *The Office* are about nothing. Life is displayed as the sum of daily trivialities, pet peeves and personal idiosyncrasies. These are funny shows. I like to watch them. They poke fun at our insidious narcissism and shared insecurities, but they tend to go beyond amusement and end up portraying an underlying philosophy of life. Sitcoms and "reality" shows cover up the loss of our meta-narrative. Having given up on the big story that makes sense of our little stories, we are left with the pieces of an anecdotal jigsaw puzzle that no longer fits together—too many pieces are missing. We are tempted to give up on the super-serious questions of life and just focus on the insignificant details of our lives.

If Nietzsche were alive today, what would he think of *The Office*? His bitterly ironic writings are the flip-side to today's seriously unserious television shows. Nietzsche's anguish has been replaced by amusement, his despair turned into a joke. He thought "that all philosophy, all religion, all science, all literature, all art were only so many desperate attempts to paint meaning on a meaningless cosmic canvas."[1] I imagine he would be shocked to find people so quick and skilled at making jokes out of a philosophy of life that led to despair and the will to power. The outcome of our philosophically defended emptiness and scientifically celebrated meaninglessness is a surprisingly good sense of humor. We're okay with meaninglessness. There is not much difference between philosophical nothingness and life about nothing. Down through the centuries Christians have affirmed the doctrine of creation *ex nihilo* (out of nothing), but *nihilism* (nothing) is more in vogue today.

Physicist Steven Weinberg claims that it is a scientific fact that the universe is meaningless. Scientists may think they are doing meaningful work—they "build telescopes and satellites and accelerators, and sit at their desks for endless hours working on the meaning of the data they gather. The effort to understand the universe is one of the very few things that lifts human life a little above the level of farce, and gives it some of the grace of tragedy."[2] From Weinberg's perspective all scientists are confused—borderline psychotic, in their search of meaning, when there is no meaning to be found. Purpose is only a figment of our imagination. Whatever appearance of meaning there may be, the universe is ultimately meaningless.

Solomon chose to explore the meaning of life from a humanistic perspective. He unpacked "the notion of wholesale pointlessness in the universe."[3] In many ways, Ecclesiastes offers an ancient perspective on a modern position. This biblical book is a carefully crafted assessment of life and work, pleasure and passion, in a world where there is no biblical history. Although the author captures the pathos of this joyless alternative so well that he seems to identify with its conclusions, he clearly intended to move the reader beyond meaninglessness and apathy to a God-centered worldview. The Teacher in Ecclesiastes made his case through the back door, but all along he was heading for this truth: "The end of the matter; all has been heard. Fear God and keep his commandments, for this is the whole duty of man. For God will bring every deed into judgment, with every secret thing, whether good or evil" (12:13–14). Let the tale of disappointment, even despair, be told in full, but when all is said and done, the Teacher advises us to turn to God as our only hope.

Ecclesiastes is a sustained argument against the meaning that human beings try to give to life, as well as a powerful apologetic for the meaning that only God can give to life. Thus Wisdom explores the experience of frustration, futility and failure in the closed universe of our own making and imagining, but also points beyond this secular despair and humanistic malaise to the gift of God.

UNDER THE SUN

The Teacher's quest for meaning is limited to life under the sun, a phrase repeated twenty-nine times. He drives his world-denying, life-negating point into our souls, but every once in a while he interjects flashes of insight that point beyond an apparently closed universe of despair. We should understand at the outset that faith in God is not something tacked on at the end of this book in order to rescue it from its blatant skepticism and cynicism.

Ecclesiastes teaches that the difference between despair and delight is absolutely singular. The one and only reality that separates us from futility and meaninglessness is the reality of God– the fear of God. This is the fear that drives out fear; the fear that is not afraid of God, but seeks to please God. This is the fear that is best translated as faith, trust, and love. The Teacher confronts all who pride themselves on their personal achievements, who confidently rely on nature alone, who take stock in their material success, and who believe that they can personally generate a sense of meaning and significance. Ecclesiastes is Wisdom's critique of all egocentric attempts to redefine the meaning of life. There is no divorce in Solomon's mind between devotional and scientific thinking. The truth he explores is fundamental to the totality of life.

From what we know of Solomon's life, he was well-suited for a rigorous assessment of life from a secular perspective. He excelled in worldly wisdom, sensual pleasure, personal achievement, material acquisition, and political power. The author writes with a conviction born of personal experience and with a passion determined to set the record straight. The author's artistic expression is commensurate with Solomon's renowned reputation, and his logical path of inquiry is consistent with his life experience.

The words of the Teacher, son of David, king in Jerusalem, are emphatic. "Meaningless! Meaningless!" says the Teacher. "Utterly meaningless! Everything is meaningless." The answer precedes the question, removing any secret as to his conclusion. "What does man gain from all his labor at which he toils under the sun?" The rhythm of the poetry belies the monotony of the endless cycle of life, and its beauty contradicts its pessimism. Everything that goes around comes around. Life is nothing more than a never-ending repetitive routine. "All things are full of weariness" (1:8). The vanity, emptiness, and weariness of life is so great that it defies our ability to describe it in words. Poets and rock stars try, but fail. Generation after generation, day after day, season after season, the meaninglessness of it all is killing us.

Life is like a syndicated re-run played over and over again. Many religions, from Native American to Buddhism, have based their world-view on this cyclical pattern of life, but the author is not about to try and develop the goal of life out of a pattern of life best symbolized by a hula-hoop. "What has been will be again, what has been done will be done again; there is nothing new under the sun." All this to say, "What's the point? Nothing matters. No one is remembered."

The one making this assertion should know, since he's the boss. "I, the Teacher, was king over Israel in Jerusalem. I devoted myself to study and to explore by wisdom all that is done under heaven. What a heavy burden God has laid on men! I have seen all the things that are done under the sun; all of them are meaningless, a chasing after wind" (1:12–14 NIV). I like the way the English Standard Version translates the Hebrew text: "It is an unhappy business that God has given to the children of man to be busy with" (1:13 ESV). The author's pejorative view of God is consistent with his limited view of wisdom. From his vantage point, under the sun, how could he not but be disappointed with God and attribute the burden of life to his Maker? Here, the secular mind is neither nihilistic nor atheistic, but deistic. God set everything in motion, but people are left to fend for themselves in a broken and burdensome world. This perspective echoes the vast majority who say they believe in God, yet live totally secular lives, and then turn around and blame God for letting them down when life doesn't turn out in their favor. Wisdom under the sun makes God out to be an imposition, laying burdens on people that they cannot bear. Many people seem to believe in God only to the extent that they blame God for the futility and frustration of their lives.

Given his narrow definition of reality, Solomon gave his verdict before making his case. He boldly declared, "I have seen all the things that are done under the sun; all of them are meaningless, a chasing after wind" (1:14 NIV). He arrived at this conclusion based on his personal experience. Drawing on his superior intelligence, undisputed power, and vast financial resources, Solomon exploited self-rule to its maximum potential. He was able to do whatever his heart desired and whatever he set his mind to accomplish. He began by pursuing education: "I applied my heart to know wisdom and to know madness and folly. I perceived that this also is but a striving after wind"(1:17). Depressed by the fact that wisdom and sorrow; knowledge and grief were in direct proportion, it is not surprising that Solomon tried to find fulfillment in having fun. "I thought in my heart, 'Come now, I will test you with pleasure to find out what is good.'" But even though he pursued pleasure and entertainment with passion, he came to the painful conclusion that it was all meaningless.

So he threw himself into work. What others could only fantasize about, Solomon accomplished on a grand scale in his very egocentric world.

> I undertook great projects: I built houses for myself and planted vineyards . . . I bought male and female slaves . . . I owned more herds and flocks than anyone in Jerusalem before me. I amassed silver and gold for myself, and the treasures of kings and provinces. I acquired men and women singers, and a harem as well—the delights of the heart of man. (2:4–8 NIV)

He excelled in three status-measuring categories—money, sex, and power. We assume that Solomon obtained his superiority without regard for the Law of God or moral sensitivity, yet it was not his conscience that bothered him, but the sheer emptiness and futility of an oppressive and hedonistic lifestyle. Solomon would have been a difficult person to eulogize if he hadn't written his own cynical epitaph: "Then I considered all that my hands had done and the toil I had expended in doing it, and behold, all was vanity and a striving after wind, and there was nothing to be gained under the sun" (2:11).

Solomon's rigorous assessment of wisdom *under the sun* drew a fatalistic conclusion: death ends all. The wise die just like the fool. What difference does it make? None. "The same fate overtakes them both" (2:14 NIV) and both "will not be long remembered" (2:16 NIV). What good is it to labor all your life with "wisdom, knowledge and skill" and then leave your hard earned success to someone who didn't lift a finger to earn it and is in all probability a fool?

Those who limit the scope of wisdom to nature alone seldom explore end-of-life issues with such blunt force and unabashed self-centeredness. There is no hint in wisdom under the sun that people are living for anything other than personal pleasure and achievement. Family has no place in the discussion. Helping others is not a consideration. Even a secular utilitarian concept, such as the greatest good for the greatest number people, is foreign. Evidently the Teacher was adamant about taking secular wisdom to its logical conclusion, with the predictable result that life under the sun was found to be meaningless (2:23). This was not an abstract philosophical conclusion for him, but an awful conviction that led to despair. "So I hated life, because the work that is done under the sun was grievous to me. All of it is meaningless, a chasing after the wind" (2:17 NIV).

GLIMPSES OF LIGHT

Solomon appears envious of the ordinary person who knows God. His graphic description of an ego-driven, self-exalted power broker is juxtaposed with a simple picture of an ordinary person who enjoys the simple pleasures of life as a gift from God. "There is nothing better for a person than that he should eat and drink and find enjoyment in his toil. This also, I saw, is from the hand of God, for apart from him who can eat or who can have enjoyment?" (2:24–25). According to Solomon, the simple God-fearing man or woman has something over Richard Dawkins and Donald Trump.

This is remarkable—an ordinary Joe has it over a master of the universe. The person who lives to please himself is confronted by the person who lives to please God. The seemingly amoral world of slavery, oppression, indulgence, and worldly success is suddenly introduced to the real world of God's blessing and judgment. "For to the one who pleases him, God has given wisdom and knowledge and joy, but to the sinner he has given the business of gathering and collecting, only to give to one who pleases God" (2:26). Nevertheless, the Teacher keeps the case for skepticism alive by cynically concluding, "This too is meaningless, a chasing after wind" (2:26 NIV).

His famous poem, "A Time for Everything," can be slanted two ways (3:1–8). Cynically, it laments the tyranny of time—a reminder that we are subject to circumstances and conditions beyond our control. Alternately, we could read it as a carefully crafted lyrical testimony to the rhythm and purpose of life. Perhaps how we interpret the meaning of this poem is a reflection of our worldview. It makes sense for wisdom under the sun to lament the tyranny of time and to conclude that blind determinism governs human affairs, but from the perspective of wisdom under God, it makes sense to celebrate the rhythm of life governed by God's providential care. Whether this poem is perceived as an echo of the repetitive cycle of life lamented earlier (1:4–9) or a comforting message extolling the virtue of God's perfect timing depends solely on the gift of God. Both poems ask, "What does the worker gain from his toil?" (3:9; see 1:3) and both passages refer to "the burden God has laid on men" (3:10; see 1:13), but the secular *under the sun* perspective in chapter one is transcended by a God-centered perspective in chapter three. The dark cloud of pessimism is lifted and the dogmatic assertion of meaninglessness is eclipsed by the work of God.

He has made everything beautiful in its time. He has also set eternity in the hearts of men; yet they cannot fathom what God has done from beginning to end. I know that there is nothing better for men than to be happy and do good while they live. That every man may eat and drink, and find satisfaction in all his toil–this is the gift of God. (Ecclesiastes 3:11–13 NIV)

The tension in Ecclesiastes lies in the contrast between a meaningless, self-centered existence and a meaningful God-centered life. True instruction is found in discerning the difference between the importance that people try to impose on life and the significance that God gives to life. The Teacher chose to use his own life story as a negative example. First, he developed his quest for significance and success, portraying its utter futility and emptiness. Then he contrasted his meaningless chasing after the wind with the gift of God quietly received by ordinary people. The message is clear. Solomon in all his glory did not compare to the God-fearing individuals who found satisfaction in their labor because of God.

Ecclesiastes challenges our strategies for success. We are admonished to re-evaluate our goals and priorities. There is a striking affinity between those who are described in Ecclesiastes as able to enjoy life because of the blessing of God and the early Christian believers who made it their ambition to lead a quiet life, to mind their own business, and to work with their hands, so that they would win the respect of outsiders (1 Thessalonians 4:11–12). The desire to shun the rat race and "live peaceful and quiet lives in all godliness and holiness" is a lesson right out of Ecclesiastes (1 Timothy 2:2). The apostle Paul's description of the believers at Corinth reinforces Solomon's perspective. "Not many of you were wise by human standards; not many were influential; not many of noble birth. But God chose the foolish things of the world to shame the wise; God chose the weak things of the world to shame the strong" (1 Corinthians 1:26–27 NIV).

Ecclesiastes challenges any notion of understanding life as we know it, from the nature of creation to interpersonal relationships apart from God. From a humanistic point-of-view, everything is meaningless. No matter how successful someone is, he dies like an animal (3:19). Solomon was decidedly pessimistic. "As everyone man comes, so they depart, and what do they gain, since they toil for the wind? All their days they eat in darkness, with great frustration, affliction and anger" (5:16–17). Solomon's perspective foreshadows the apostle Paul's conviction when he declared, "If only for this life we have hope in Christ, we are to be pitied more than all people" (1 Corinthians 15:19)?

The Teacher's critical analysis of life under the sun results in a long hard look at the mess of the human condition. He sweeps aside all the easy answers, political spin, and psycho-babble that might blunt his critique of our fallen evil world. Like an oncologist examining a patient, or a detective examining a crime scene, he is determined to get to the bottom of this and expose the depravity of the human condition.

Solomon's critique is more like the stanzas of a modern rock song than a lecture on evil. It's definitely not a logical journal article or a legal brief. Ecclesiastes reads like the printed words on a CD jacket. They are cutting and provocative, designed to evoke the pathos of our depravity and expose the futility of our lives. Through much of the book, Solomon keeps God at a distance. The mess of the human condition is in the forefront and the mystery of God is in the background. As we might expect from one who pursued his own course with such selfish passion, Solomon tended to refer to God in impersonal terms.

SECOND THOUGHTS FOR SKEPTICS

The perspective of abiding faith in God breaks in at critical points, but only after the remoteness of God is painfully felt. Whenever the author limited his field of vision to life under the sun, God is presented as a distant and remote figure. The more personal name for God, Yahweh, is never used in Ecclesiastes. It is a somewhat impersonal Creator God who will eventually judge the righteous and the wicked, and who will hold people accountable for their vowed commitments. But in the present, secular wisdom perceives a distant deity divorced from man's desperate situation. From a humanistic point-of-view, everything is meaningless.

In the debate between wisdom under the sun and wisdom from God, skepticism gets the most "air time." Cynicism rules the debate. The main message is "Meaningless!" and it comes through loud and clear. The Teacher continues his litany against humanity's sorry state: "I have seen another evil under the sun, and it weighs heavily on men: God gives a man wealth, possessions and honor, so that he lacks nothing his heart desires, but God does not enable him to enjoy them, and a stranger enjoys them instead. This is meaningless, a grievous evil" (6:1–2). The skeptic responds to the good news of the gift of God by arguing that God withholds his grace arbitrarily. A person could have a hundred children and live many years, but end up worse off than a stillborn child if he could not enjoy his prosperity (6:3–6). The Teacher seems to imply that a whimsical God is to blame for human sorrow, but then he argues that men and women don't deserve to enjoy what they have. "Everyone's toil is for the mouth, yet the appetite is never satisfied" (6:7). Face it. Life is tragic. " The day of death [is] better than the day of birth...Sorrow is better than laughter, because a sad face is good for the heart. The heart of the wise is in the house of

mourning, but the heart of fools is in the house of pleasure."
(7:2–4).

For brief moments at a time, the author's faith perspective
shines through in spite of his depressing account of life under
the sun. We are reminded that there is more to life than the
mess of the human condition. Life's goodness is God's gift.
"Then I realized that it is good and proper for people to eat and
drink, and to find satisfaction in their toilsome labor under the
sun during the few days of life God has given them—for this is
their lot. Moreover, when God gives people wealth and possessions, and the ability to enjoy them, to accept their lot and be
happy in their toil—this is a gift of God" (5:18–19). The joy of
living is found in the gift of God, and not, as many would have
us think, in personal achievement. God alone makes the difference between receiving life as a blessing or turning life into
a burden. It is not the meaning that we bring to life, but the
meaning that God gives to life that makes all the difference and
brings joy. Solomon recognized that the person who receives
the gift of God is not overwhelmed by the human condition,
but freed up to enjoy life. "He seldom reflects on the days of his
life, because God keeps him occupied with gladness of heart"
(5:20). The mystery of God shines through this bleak account of
human existence and reminds us once again that there is more
to life than oppression, injustice, and death.

Solomon was insistent that we face the harsh realities of life
coming our way and turn to God. "Remember your Creator
in the days of your youth, before the days of trouble come
and the years approach when you say, 'I find no pleasure in
them'" (12:1). Solomon likened the ravages of old age to a house
falling apart. The crystal chandelier has crashed, the pipes are
breaking and the plaster is peeling. Nothing works anymore.

Solomon made his point eloquently. Eventually, everything fails us. "'Meaningless! Meaningless!' says the Teacher. 'Everything is meaningless!'"

Ecclesiastes is much more than a lecture against self-sufficiency. It is a relentless attack against any notion that we can generate meaning and significance for ourselves. The Teacher painstakingly works out the practical meaning of total depravity and helps us to see what life is really like under the sun. Perhaps the well-ordered, confident optimism of Proverbs fits our family life, but Ecclesiastes definitely fits the corporate office, urban neighborhood, and suburban high school. By the time Ecclesiastes is through with us, we have our pride exposed and our secular strategies of success deflated. The Teacher helps us to understand our misguided secular outlook on life and our ignorant insistence on living as if God didn't count. Solomon referred to his pointed words of wisdom as goads prodding us to pay attention and nails pinning the truth down so we can lay hold of it.

However, the Teacher was careful to explain that the source for this wisdom was not himself, but it was "given by one Shepherd" (12:11). He implies that the Creator God is not distant and impersonal afterall, but personally present to shepherd us in the truth. God is the author of these truths that reveal the tragedy of living by and for one's self. God is the judge of these little "masters of the universe" whose lives are meaningless. It is God, not just Solomon, that insists that we take a long hard look at life under the sun. And if we persist in living one dimensional lives we have only ourselves to blame for the consequences.

THE GIFT OF MEANING

Every once in a while, one hears a confessing Christian say something to the effect that life with Christ is so great that *even if it isn't true,* it would be worthwhile believing in it anyway. Solomon's rigorous quest for truth cleared the way of all distractions so that the stark contrast between the mess of the human condition and the mystery of God could be clearly seen. His whole point was that life apart from God doesn't offer a shred of meaning. Meaning comes not from an act of will, but an act of grace. It is the gift of God, "so that no one can boast" (Ephesians 2:8).

Solomon was dogmatic: apart from the God-given gift of meaning there is no hope! God alone builds meaning into life and enables us to experience joy. What Solomon could not have envisioned was how much God would give of himself to create a meaningful life. Nor could he have ever fathomed the unique and hidden character of this central truth. The Incarnation of God is the ultimate truth of a meaningful world. "The Word was made flesh and dwelt among us and we have seen his glory, the glory of the only begotten of the Father full of grace and truth" (John 1:14). How could Solomon have ever anticipated the price of our redemption and the gift of everlasting life? "For God so loved the world that he gave his one and only Son, that whoever believes in him shall not perish but have eternal life" (John 3:16). If Solomon depended by faith on these relatively faint and early manifestations of the gift of God, how much more should we embrace the gift of God's grace revealed in Christ's cross and resurrection! "For it is by grace you have been saved, through faith, and this not from yourselves, it is the gift of God—not by works, so that no one can boast" (Ephesians

2:8–10). "Thanks be to God for his indescribable gift!" (2 Corinthians 9:15).

Think of Ecclesiastes as the opening lecture in Physics 101. We can't do science without thinking through the issues raised by the Teacher. Even science, in the restricted sense of the scientific enterprise, that limits inquiry to phenomenon that is observable, repeatable, and transferable, cannot proceed without a foundation that validates the human capacity to analyze the data. In other words, we cannot do science without epistemology. Paradoxically, the truth that some disparage as subjective knowledge, that is, a kind of soft knowing based on emotion and intuition rather than empirical fact, is the very bedrock objective knowledge necessary for comprehending the phenomenal world. As long as science is processed by a person we cannot avoid the issues raised by the Teacher. If we try to relegate the concerns raised in this book to the Arts and Humanities, they will nevertheless haunt the science class. To pretend that knowledge is limited to those things we can measure and that humans are evolutionary gods is to insist on the wrong humility. Physics begs the metaphysical question. Inevitably the Who-Question trumps the What, When, and Where Questions. Solomon came to understand that epistemologies that depend upon proof are exercises in futility.

2

MERE MORTALS

"When I consider your heavens, the work of your
fingers, the moon and the stars, which you have set in
place, what are mere mortals that you are mindful
of them, human beings that you care for them?"

Psalm 8:3–4

At the heart of this psalm of creation is a question: "What are mere mortals that you are mindful of them, human beings that you care for them?" David answers the question by revealing the significance of humanity from four God-centered perspectives. Human identity and worth are discovered in relationship to God's majesty (8:1–2), God's cosmos (8:3–4), God's calling (8:5–8); and God's praise (8:9). This theological truth is just as valid scientifically as it is devotionally.

The basic question of the Psalm is asked in different ways. In Psalm 144, David's slant is pessimistic: "O Lord, what is man that you care for him, the son of man that you think of him? Man is like a breath; his days are like a fleeting shadow" (Psalm 144:3). Job agonizes before God over a significance he wishes he didn't have: "What is man that you make so much of him, that

31

you give him so much attention, that you examine him every morning and test him every moment?" (Job 7:17–18).

In *The Question of God,* Armand Nicholi, professor of clinical psychiatry at Harvard Medical School, writes,

> Socrates said 'the unexamined life is not worth living.' Within the university, students and professors scrutinize every possible aspect of our universe—from the billions of galaxies to subatomic particles, electrons, quarks—but they assiduously avoid examining their own lives. In the wider world, we keep hectically busy and fill every free moment of our day with some form of diversion—work, computers, television, movies, radio, magazines, newspapers, sports, alcohol, drugs, parties. Perhaps we distract ourselves because looking at our lives confronts us with our lack of meaning, our unhappiness, and our loneliness—and with the difficulty, the fragility, and the unbelievable brevity of life.[1]

David asks the question that we should be asking, but he does not answer the question by lecturing us. Instead, he leads us in worship and prayer. "This psalm is an unsurpassed example of what a hymn should be, celebrating as it does the glory and grace of God, rehearsing who He is and what He has done, and relating us and our world to Him; all with a masterly economy of words, and in a spirit of mingled joy and awe."[2]

GOD'S MAJESTY: STARTING POINT OR BY-PRODUCT?

Mark Steyn wisely observed, *"The 'who' is the best indicator of what-where-when-why."*[3] The life of humankind revolves around the living God. David begins with the majesty of God. In doing so, he has chosen the essential starting point, not only for worship, but for wisdom, work, and science. He begins with the *who* in order to explain the *what-where-when-why*. "You have set your glory...You have ordained praise...You have made him a little lower than the heavenly being...You have made him ruler over the works of your hands...You put everything under his feet." For the author of Psalm 8, life itself depends upon a relationship with God; for Richard Dawkins, the author of *The God Delusion*, religion is a by-product of a quest for survival. Dawkins argues that the perceived need for religion is related to Darwinian survival. Children are dependent upon the advice of their parents for protection and well-being. From one generation to another need-to-know knowledge, necessary for survival, is mixed up with useless superstitious perspectives. Sense and nonsense are passed down from one generation to another.[4]

Dawkins argues that religion is the by-product of a deeply ingrained psychological disposition to trust others and the inability to distinguish what is real and unreal. The "useful programmability" and "gullibility" of a child's brain accounts for religion being passed down from one generation to the next. The reason moths fly directly into the candle flame is because they are genetically hardwired to use moonlight to fly a straight line. Artificial light is a relatively recent phenomenon and the number of moths killed by flying directly into the flame is rare compared to the number of moths guided by moon-light. For Dawkins, religion is a by-product of genetic hardwiring that predisposes us to believe in the authority of an older generation. He also believes that religion makes about as much sense as a moth flying directly into the flames.

C.S. Lewis came to faith in Christ in his early thirties. If there was anyone who was not programmed to believe in God and did not deserve to be labeled gullible, it was Lewis. "The things I assert most vigorously," wrote Lewis, "are those that

I resisted long and accepted late."[5] He concluded, "Christians are wrong, but all the rest are bores." Nevertheless he was searching and the more he searched the more vulnerable he felt. He likened his conversion to a chess match in which his "Adversary" broke down his defenses and outmaneuvered him. Friendship with Christians like J.R.R. Tolkien and Charles Williams had an impact on his mind's grasp of reality and his heart's yearning. He realized that no state of mind and body could satisfy his desires. He longed for something other than himself, for something outside of himself. "I did not yet ask," explains Lewis, "*Who* is the desired? only *What* is it? But this brought me already into the region of awe, for I thus understood that in deepest solitude there is a road out of the self, a commerce with something which, by refusing to identify with any object of the senses, or anything whereof we have biological or social need, or anything imagined, or any state of our own minds, proclaims itself sheerly objective."[6]

He recalls sitting on a bus going up Headington Hill in Oxford when he became very conscious of making a choice. He claims he was moved neither by desire nor fear. He was unaware of any motive or necessity. He simply chose to be open, "to unbuckle, to loosen the rein." As he said later, "Really, a young Atheist cannot guard his faith too carefully. Dangers lie in wait for him on every side. You must not do, you must not even try to do, the will of the Father unless you are prepared to 'know the doctrine.'"[7]

"Remember," Lewis admits, "I had always wanted, above all things, not to be *interfered with*. I had wanted (mad wish) *to call my soul my own*." But now Lewis had gone well beyond intellectual calculations and debate. He was no longer negotiating a treaty with God. Since God is God, nothing less than "total surrender" was called for. "The demand was not even 'All or nothing'... Now the demand was simply 'All.'" At the age of thirty-one, Lewis "gave in, and admitted that God was God."[8]

Psalm 8 is the worshiper's response to Genesis one:

> Then God said, 'Let us make man in our image, after our likeness. And let them have dominion over the fish of the sea and over the birds of the heavens and over the livestock and over all the earth and over every creeping thing that creeps on the earth. So God created man in his own image, in the image of God he created him; male and female he created them. (Genesis 1:26–27 ESV).

We are not the product of a solitary God, but the personal creation of the living God who is essentially social. At the core of our human identity is a capacity to relate to God and to one another like no other creature in creation, and this capacity is based on the being of God who is already a communion of persons. There is no impersonal *what*, only *a three-in-one who*. In other words, there is no *what* before or independent of the *who*.

There is nothing impersonal or individualistic about God, because God can only be known through his own personal self-disclosure. Thus, there is no explanation prior to the simple, straightforward revelation of God, "Let us make man in our image." God, by virtue of his own threefold being in communion, cannot be anything other than Father, Son and Spirit. Thus there is no model or affinity in God our Maker for the highly touted modern and postmodern quest for the self-actualized individual self. Autonomous individualism has no basis in the being of God, but true personal fulfillment in community does.

This is how we take after God's own image. We are relational beings and we were meant to be in relationship with the Lord God and with one another. John Stott expresses this well when he writes, "Our neighbor is neither a bodyless soul that we should love only his soul, nor a soulless body that we should care for its welfare alone, nor even a body-soul isolated from society. God created man, who is my neighbor, a body-soul-in-community."[9]

We were not meant to be autonomous individual selves, becoming our own little god, intent on living for ourselves and pleasing ourselves. Loneliness is a painful symptom of the primary problem of sin, that personal act of defiance against the God who made us and loves us. Sin separates us from God and his creation and drives a wedge through every relationship. Sin makes us feel like castaways and turns life into a quest for survival.

SALVATION OR SURVIVAL?

In the movie *Castaway*, actor Tom Hanks plays Chuck Nolan, an efficiency expert for FedEx. His life consists of work, which he does virtually 24/7, and a relationship with a girlfriend. Just before he boards a FedEx flight to the South Pacific he proposes to her. He kisses her goodbye and assures her he'll be back in a week, but his plane goes down in a terrible storm and he washes up on a deserted island. He is the lone survivor and a modern day version of Robinson Crusoe. The differences between the movie *Castaway* and Daniel Defoe's novel *Robinson Crusoe* help to illustrate the gap between two radically different views of the human person.

Castaway is a movie that looks at Chuck Nolan's struggle to survive, while *Robinson Crusoe* is a novel that explores the mind and soul of Crusoe. Perhaps a novel can capture the inner workings of the soul better than a movie. In *Castaway*, we watch a familiar star act out a part. We comment to ourselves that Hanks looks heavy in the first half of the movie and about fifty pounds lighter in the second half of the movie. We make a mental note of his bleached hair and beard. From the odd assortment of FedEx packages that wash up on shore we question the value of our materialism. We watch him try to build a fire out of rubbing sticks and extract a tooth with the tip of an ice-skate. The only clue to what is on his mind is his habit of looking at his girlfriend's picture and his attempts to draw her likeness on the wall of a cave. When the body of the pilot washes up on shore, Nolan digs a shallow grave and buries the body. He stands before the mound, but instead of prayer, all he says is, "That's that." The portrayal is entirely one-dimensional. It is a tale of survival. When Nolan's bloody hand print leaves the imprint of a face on a volleyball, he names it "Wilson." The ensuing dialogue between Nolan and Wilson is both humorous and sad, and symbolic of what the secular mind thinks of prayer.

As the years drag on, Nolan contemplates suicide and becomes more like a caveman than a FedEx efficiency expert. He just barely clings to survival. As a last ditch effort, Nolan builds a raft and sails out to sea to an almost certain death if it were not for the lucky break of being spotted by an ocean tanker. He arrives home after a four-year absence to find his fiancee married. He has survived, but he cannot redeem the lost years and the lost relationships. The movie closes with Nolan standing at a four cornered crossroads in the middle of the Texas panhandle as lost and directionless as he was on his deserted South Pacific island.

Castaway and *Robinson Crusoe* develop two contrasting pictures. In Defoe's novel, Crusoe emerges from his nearly three decades of isolation a much stronger person than he was at the beginning. His isolation proved invaluable. In the providence of God, his solitary life led him to examine himself. Suffering opened his heart and mind to God. Stripped of everything worldly, he saw himself as he really was, "without desire of good or conscience of evil." He began to lament his "stupidity of soul" and his ingratitude to God.[10] Illness led him to pray for the first time in years, "Lord be my help, for I am in great distress." When he began to ask, "Why has God done this to me? What have I done to deserve this?" His conscience checked him, "Wretch! Ask what you have done! Look back upon a dreadful misspent life and ask what you have done. Ask, why you have not been destroyed long before this!"[11]

Robinson Crusoe is more about salvation than survival. Like the prodigal son, who ran off to the far country and squandered his inheritance, Crusoe comes to his senses. He is deeply convinced and convicted of his wickedness. He turns to the Lord and prays for help in repenting of his sins. Providentially, he reads in the Bible, "God exalted him to his own right hand as Prince and Savior that he might give repentance and forgiveness of sins to Israel" (Acts 5:31). He describes his reaction, "I threw down the book, and with all my heart as well as my hands lifted up to Heaven, in a kind of ecstasy of joy, I cried out aloud, 'Jesus, Thou Son of David, Jesus, Thou exalted Prince and Savior, give me repentance!'" Instead of praying for physical deliverance he prayed for the forgiveness of his sins. Deliverance from sin was "a much greater blessing than deliverance from affliction."[12]

He comes to the sober conclusion that his soul's salvation meant far more to him than his deliverance from isolation. "I began to conclude in my mind that it was possible for me to be more happy in this forsaken, solitary condition than it was probable I should ever have been in any other particular state in the world; and with this thought I was going to give thanks to God for bringing me to this place."[13] Instead of a slow and fearful descendent into despair, Crusoe experienced God's rhythms of grace. He read his Bible and prayed daily. He planted crops, made furniture, baked bread, built a canoe, and established an orderly, disciplined life. He lived a life of mercy, not sorrow, and his singular goal was to "make my sense of God's mercy to me."

The message of *Castaway* is that life is a solitary struggle for survival fueled by the human spirit and the existential self. Love, particularly romantic love, can be a great motivator, but relationships are often disappointing and not enduring. Loneliness and isolation expose the myths of modern life, and in the end we are directionless. The message of *Robinson Crusoe* is that life is a struggle in our soul between self-rule and God's will, and it can only come to resolution by the grace and mercy of God. Apart from the saving grace of the Lord Jesus Christ there is no hope, but with Christ we can experience an abundant life even in affliction and suffering.

GOD'S COSMOS: HUMILITY OR HUMILIATION?

Theologian Carl Henry offers a line worth pondering: "Human reason is a divinely fashioned instrument for recognizing truth; it is not a creative source of truth."[14] The psalmist would have agreed. Against the cosmic canopy, David felt small: "I look up at your macro-skies, dark and enormous, your handmade sky-jewelry, moon and stars mounted in their settings. Then I look at my micro-self and wonder, Why do you bother with us? Why take a second look our way?" (Psalm 8, The Message).

If David felt insignificant in comparison with the vastness of the universe, how much more should we, who are familiar with modern cosmology, feel our littleness? An astrophysicist can describe the earth as an insignificant speck of dust in the vastness of the universe, a tiny planet, revolving around a mediocre star on the outskirts of the Milky Way. And the Milky Way is just one galaxy of millions of galaxies, each separated by about a million light years. But earth is our home; a place of beauty and meaning. In a universe of one hundred billion trillion stars this is the only place we can live, making earth very valuable real estate. As we look at the universe we ought to be impressed with the scandal of significance! "What is man, Lord, that you are mindful of him, the son of man that you care for him?" Of all living creatures, the human person is the most unique, gifted with capacities to think, to love, to create, to reflect, and to communicate. Of all places, earth is the most unique, gifted with a finely balanced eco-system—the only place where we can live.

The most real world is not the world of our making, but of our receiving. The most real world is not the music world, the entertainment world, the financial world, the sports world or the academic world. The most real world is God's creation. David wants us to see the largeness of God against the competing bigness of the world. There is a great deal that threatens to distort, even destroy this perspective: the routine grind of daily living, the pressure to earn one's livelihood, the fascination with technology, the problems and pace of modern living—all these can blunt our sense of the wonder of God's creation.

There is a right way to feel insignificant and a wrong way to feel insignificant. Knowing the difference is critical for our self-understanding. The praise of God rightly provokes a sense of smallness. Human depravity wrongly imposes a sense of worthlessness. God's Holiness challenges our unwarranted self-confidence and commends our true worth.

Sigmund Freud reduced man to the fear of death and the desire for sex. Karl Marx reduced man to the means of production and the class struggle. Charles Darwin reduced man to the fight for survival and the urge to propagate. British physicist and biochemist Francis Crick, who along with James D. Watson discovered the molecular structure of DNA, offers this perspective on the human person:

> The Astonishing Hypothesis is that 'You,' your joys and your sorrows, your memories and your ambitions, your sense of personal identity and free will, are in fact no more than the behavior of a vast assembly of nerve cells and their associated molecules. . . .
>
> I have described the general workings of an intricate machine—the brain—that handles an immense amount of information all at once, in one perceptual moment...The mysterious aspects of consciousness might disappear, just as the mysterious aspects of embryology have largely disappeared now that we know about the capabilities of DNA, RNA, and protein...Only scientific certainty (with all its limitations) can in the long run rid us of the superstitions of our ancestors.
>
> This new knowledge [as opposed to the myths and superstitions of the past] has not diminished our sense of awe but increased it immeasurably...The psalmist said, 'I am fearfully and wonderfully made,' but he had a very indirect glimpse of the delicate and sophisticated nature of our molecular construction. The processes of evolution have produced wonders of which our civilized ancestors had no knowledge at all....To say that our behavior is based on a vast, interacting assembly of neurons should not diminish our view of ourselves but enlarge it tremendously.[15]

R. Buckminster Fuller describes *Homo sapiens* (literally, *wise man*) as an ingenious machine. He pictures the human person as:

> a self-balancing, 28 jointed, adapter-based biped, an electro-chemical reduction plant, integral with the segregated storages of special energy extracts in storage batteries, for the subsequent actuation of thousands of hydraulic and pneumatic pumps, with motors attached; 62,000 miles of capillaries, millions of warning signals, railroad and conveyor systems; crushers and cranes . . . and a universally distributed telephone system needing no service for seventy years if well managed: the whole extraordinary complex mechanism guided with exquisite precision from a turret in which are located telescopic and microscopic self-registering and recording range finders, a spectroscope, et cetera.[16]

Loren Eiseley, describes man as the zenith of the evolutionary process. In his Encyclopedia Britannica article, entitled *The Cosmic Orphan* he writes:

> The thing that is you bears the still-aching wounds of evolution in body and in brain. Your hands are made-over fins, your lungs come from a swamp, your femur has been twisted upright. Your feet is a reworked climbing pad. You are a rag doll resown from the skins of extinct animals. Long ago, 2 million years perhaps, you were smaller; your brain was not so large. We are not confident that you could speak. Seventy million years before that you were an even smaller climbing creature . . . .You were the size of a rat. You ate insects. Now you fly to the moon.[17]

Alexander Pope's *Essay on Man* sought to limit the inquiry:

> Know then thyself, presume not God to scan; the proper study of mankind is man. Placed on this isthmus of a middle state, being darkly wise and rudely great; with too much knowledge for the skeptic side, with too much weakness for the stoic's pride, he hangs between; in doubt to act, or rest; in doubt to

deem himself a God, or beast; in doubt his mind or body to
prefer . . . Sole judge of Truth, in Endless hurled: The glory, jest
and riddle of the world![18]

From ancient history to modern times, the human race has
tried to counter reductionistic conclusions about human worth
and value and create its own significance. The tower of Babel
was one such attempt. Fearing failure, the people of Shinar said,
"Come, let us build ourselves a city, with a tower that reaches
to the heavens, so that we may make a name for ourselves and
not be scattered over the face of the whole earth" (Genesis11:4).
This human experiment in self-engineered greatness ended in
judgment.

Ironically, the late Carl Sagan, in his book, *A Pale Blue Dot*,
envisions thousands of years from now our descendants will be
scattered throughout the cosmos, peopling other worlds. They
"will gaze up and strain to find the blue dot in their skies."
They will "marvel at how vulnerable the repository of all our
potential once was, how perilous our infancy, how humble
our beginnings, how many rivers we had to cross before we
found our way."[19] Carl Sagan envisions an achieved significance
realized through pioneering planetary space travel and settle-
ment.

French mathematician and Christian apologist Blaise Pascal
wisely observed the impact of reductionistic views of humanity:
"Man is so made that if he is told often enough that he is a fool
he believes it. By telling himself so often enough he convinces
himself, because when he is alone he carries on an inner
dialogue with himself which it is important to keep under
proper control. Evil communications corrupt good manners.
We must keep silent as far as we can and only talk to ourselves

about God, whom we know to be true, and thus convince ourselves that he is."[20]

Pascal believed that it was impossible for human beings to understand themselves apart from knowing God. Explore the human person psychologically, physiologically, sociologically, and you will not have gotten a true picture of humanity. What John Calvin wrote in 1536 remains true:

> Our wisdom, in so far as it ought to be deemed true and solid wisdom, consists almost entirely of two parts: the knowledge of God and of ourselves...no person can survey himself without immediately turning his thoughts towards the God in whom he lives and moves; because it is perfectly obvious, that the endowments which we possess cannot possibly be from ourselves... It is evident that a person never attains to a true self-knowledge until she has previously contemplated the face of God, and come down after such contemplation to look into herself....the knowledge of God and the knowledge of ourselves are bound together by a mutual tie.[21]

GOD'S CALL: BLESSING OR BURDEN?

We do not need to make something of ourselves. Self-worth is not a human achievement. We are endowed with value and meaning. Significance is built-in. By virtue of the fact that we are made in God's image, the value of the person is not optional. Not only were we created in God's image but we were mandated to exercise wise stewardship over God's creation (Genesis 1:26). God blessed humanity with these words: "Be fruitful and multiply and fill the whole earth and subdue it and have dominion over the fish of the sea and the birds of the air and over every living thing that moves on the earth" (Genesis 1:28 ESV).

David's purpose in praying Psalm 8 was to revel in the wonder and glory of God's creation. David raises the question, "What is man?" without a "tinge of pessimism; only astonishment that 'you are mindful' and 'you care.'"[22] But we know there is more to the description of man than what David covers in Psalm 8. We go from the greatness of God to the littleness of man, and then from the significance of man to the sinfulness of man.

What a strange, bewildering paradox! Capable of great good, culpable of great evil, extraordinary creativity, unbelievable cruelty. Humanity suffers this painful schizophrenia; we are all like Dr. Jekyll and Mr. Hyde. Hamlet's soliloquy seems to follow Psalm 8 by first looking at the cosmos and then man, but the result is despair, not wonder:

> I have of late—but wherefore I know not—lost all my mirth, foregone all custom of exercises; and, indeed, it goes so heavily with my disposition that this goodly frame, the earth, seems to me a sterile promontory; this most excellent canopy, the air, look you, this brave overhanging firmament, this majestical roof fretted with golden fire,—why, it appears no other thing to me than a foul and pestilent congregation of vapors.
>
> What a piece of work is man! how noble in reason! how infinite in faculty! in form and motion how expressive and admirable! in action how like an angel! in apprehension how like a god! the beauty of the world! the paragon of animals! And yet, to me, what is this quintessence of dust? man delights not me; no, nor woman neither.[23]

Pascal was right, "True religion would have to teach greatness and wretchedness, inspire self-esteem and self-contempt, love and hate."[24]

THE SON OF MAN

Psalm 8 relates to the whole of mankind, but it finds its true focus pre-eminently in him who is uniquely the Son of Man and in whom alone the sinfulness of humankind is healed. The early church quoted Psalm 8 to reflect a new interpretation. What David applied to humanity in general was now applied to Jesus specifically. For he "has put everything under his feet." Now when it says that "everything" has been put under him, it is clear that this does not include God himself, who put everything under Christ" (1 Corinthians 15:27). "And God placed all things under his feet and appointed him to be head over everything for the church..." (Ephesians 1:22).

We have been led by David to see the greatness of God, the littleness of man and the significance of man. We have been led by the early church's interpretation of Psalm 8 to see the sinfulness of man and our need for the Son of Man. Humankind yearns for true significance and the power to overcome sinfulness. In Christ we discover the difference between humiliation and humility before God; the difference between the arrogance of pretending to be masters of the universe, and the humility of being stewards of the Lord of the universe.

We have framed the question, "What is man?" as David has, with praise to God. From the cosmos to children, God reveals his strength and majesty. From the grand scale of the universe to the grandchild; from one hundred billion galaxies and counting, to the kids on the block; from the immensity of the cosmos to the infant in the crib, may Jesus Christ be praised! Psalm 8 begins and ends with doxology: "O Lord, our Lord, how majestic is your name in all the earth." Biology and anthropology begin and end with Theology. David could not have agreed more. He lifts our eyes to the wonder and mystery of God's creation—as does the writer of Hebrews: "By faith we understand that the universe was formed at God's command, so that what is seen was not made out of what was visible" (Hebrews 11:3).

Twelve years after his conversion to Christ, C.S. Lewis preached a sermon entitled *The Weight of Glory* at Oxford University Church of St. Mary the Virgin. In his sermon he explored what it meant for those in Christ to share in God's glory. He exposed "the evil enchantment of worldliness" which conditions us to think that death ends all and that all that matters is what we find here on earth.

> Almost our whole education has been directed to silencing this shy, persistent, inner voice; almost all our modern philosophies have been devised to convince us that the good of man is to be found on this earth. And yet it is a remarkable thing that such philosophies of Progress or Creative Evolution themselves bear reluctant witness to the truth that our real goal is elsewhere.[25]

We have a destination outside of the limitations of this world's space and time. We rub shoulders with people destined for heaven or hell. We have never met a mere mortal.

In the midst of his hellish suffering, Job fought his way to the conclusion that human existence was more than chance and fate, and a few short years of pleasure and pain. He wanted the truth of God and his own destiny engraved on his soul. Although he was crushed, he clung to one enduring hope. "Oh, that my words were recorded, that they were written on a scroll, that they were inscribed with an iron tool on lead, or engraved in rock forever! I know that my Redeemer lives, and that in the end he will stand on earth. And after my skin has been destroyed, yet in my flesh I will see God; I myself will see him with my own eyes—I, and not another. How my heart yearns with me!" (Job 19:23–27).

This is not devotional truth alone. Job's message is essential truth for philosophy, history, biology, and theology. Sooner or later we all suffer, and when we do, we have to choose between nature alone or the God of nature. We have to choose between Jesus and Nietzsche, or Jesus and Oprah, or Jesus and Dawkins. The choice is not between Faith and Science, but between the majesty of God and the futility of human existence apart from God.

3

THE ULTIMATE KNOWER

"Now I know in part; then I shall know
fully, even as I am fully known."

1 Corinthians 13:12

S elf-understanding is not something we can do alone. The success of social networking sites such as *Facebook* or *LinkedIn* only makes sense in a relational world. We are social creatures and our primary knowledge is relational. Identity is forged in community. Every truly self-aware person discovers "that in the deepest solitude there is a road out of self."[1] We do not understand ourselves by studying inanimate objects, impersonal forces, biological theories, and mathematical equations. As important as these studies may be, they do not reveal the truth about ourselves. Nor do we know our true selves by dwelling on our feelings and wishes, our hopes and dreams. Self-understanding is not a matter of knowing as much as being known.

Meaning is not found in information alone, but in relation-ship. This is why love is the most important form of knowledge. In the Bible there is a dynamic relationship between love and knowledge, as illustrated by the apostle Paul. "This is my prayer:

that your love may abound more and more in knowledge and depth of insight, so that you may be able to discern what is best and may be pure and blameless for the day of Christ Jesus, filled with the fruit of righteousness" (Philippians 1:9–11). The expression "to know" in the Old Testament is more than a euphemism for sex. It is a telling reference to the totality of marriage and a reminder that God's primary purpose for marriage is not reproduction but relationship. In 1 Corinthians 13, the well-known Love Chapter, the apostle Paul explains what it means to grow up. "When I was a child, I talked like a child, I thought like a child, I reasoned like a child. When I became an adult, I put the ways of childhood behind me. For now we see only a reflection as in a mirror; then we shall see face to face. Now I know in part; then I shall know fully, even as I am fully known."

Children focus on a *sensory world* that can be seen, heard, touched, smelled, and tasted. Adults focus on a *sensible world* that calls for investigation, interpretation, reflection and action. Children are meant to grow up in an adult world where they are known, loved and cared for by adults. They need to be nursed, fed, protected and most of all, loved. Their growth and maturity depends on *being known better than they know.* What is true for children is also true for adults. We need to be known better than we know. Knowledge is not an autonomous exercise. Life's learning curve, "Now I know in part; then I shall know fully," depends on being "fully known." Facts can be received and data processed, but ultimately what is important is not what we know, but that we're known, and that we know that we are known. *Knowledge limited to sensory experience, to the empirical world of the five senses, is not the most important form of knowledge.* This is why we are told over and over again that the fear of the Lord is the beginning of wisdom. Divine revelation is foundational to both relational and scientific knowledge. Wisdom is the ability to see the world and ourselves from God's perspective.

Freud claims in *The Future of an Illusion* (1928) that a parent-child relationship is responsible for the illusion of God.

> When the growing individual finds that he is destined to remain a child forever, that he can never do without protection against strange superior powers, he lends those powers the features belonging to the figure of this father; he creates for himself the gods whom he dreads, whom he seeks to propitiate, and whom he nevertheless entrusts with his own protection. Thus, his longing for a father is identical with his need for protection against the consequences of human weakness.[2]

The apostle Paul and Psalm 139 claim just the opposite. The parent-child relationship is at best but a faint, albeit tender, reflection of God's abiding parental love. The choice between a world of our making and the world of God's creating is ours. Either the Creator creates creation or creation creates the creator. In a multitude of practical ways we choose between being Me-centered or God-centered. Regardless of how brilliant the scientist or philosopher may be, the insistence on a knowledge that is independent of God, is not unlike the two year old who insists on doing it himself.

To know yourself is to know in the depth of your being that you are fully known by your Maker and Redeemer. "O Lord, you have searched me and you know me." Knowing that you are fully known is the ground for knowledge and understanding. Psalm 139 describes God's parental love for us. I remember first being impressed with this psalm when our youngest child, Kennerly, was born. She was born on Wednesday, February 20,

1985, and on the following Sunday I preached on Psalm 139.
More than most fathers I was humbled by her birth, even as
I was humbled by God's previous provision in the adoption of
our two sons. I had been told that, due to my surgery for cancer
it was highly unlikely that I would be able to conceive a child. In
time, my wife Virginia and I pursued adoption and God wonderfully provided Jeremiah and Andrew for us. And then, after
ten years of marriage, Virginia became pregnant with Kennerly.
Each of our children has been a reminder of God's parental love
and that we are his children. I am known better than I know.

There is nothing like the birth of a child to make a mockery
of the belief in nature alone. I stood in a delivery room and held
our seven-pound newborn, and I was overwhelmed by the sheer
glory of her. The birth of a child causes us to re-examine the
meaning of life, to contemplate God's sovereignty and to feel
our dependence upon God. A child's dependence on human
parents is so obvious; our dependence upon God is so real.

The Lord God's knowledge of me is complete. It is intimate,
immediate, comprehensive, persistent and sovereign.

> O Lord...you know when I sit and when I rise;
>> you perceive my thoughts from afar.
> You discern my going out and my lying down;
>> you are familiar with all my ways.
> Before a word is on my tongue
>> you know it completely, O LORD. (139:1–4)

The psalmist takes comfort in the fact that God is all knowing
("You discern my going out and my lying down; you are familiar
with all my ways."), ever-present ("You hem me in, behind and
before; you have laid your hand on me. Such knowledge is too
wonderful for me, too lofty for me to attain."), totally sovereign
("All the days ordained for me were in your book before one of

them came to be"), and completely *holy*. Psalm 139 rejoices in the personal, intimate nature of this knowledge. The deeper our worship and the closer our communion with God the more we realize that the Lord knows us from the inside out. It is very freeing to be truly known and understood, accepted and loved. In spite of our sin and because of God's great mercy, we are invited into his fellowship which sustains and supports us. We are not cosmic orphans or the masters of the universe but we are the children of God.

> You hem me in—behind and before;
> you have laid your hand on me.
> Such knowledge is too wonderful for me,
> too lofty for me to attain. (139:5–6)

I cannot escape this relationship, nor do I want to. It is this relationship that defines me, secures me and understands me. Within it I am free to "rise on the wings of the dawn" or "settle on the far side of the sea" (139:9), but I am never independent from God's guidance or protection. God is the answer to my inherent fears of anonymity and loneliness. The Lord God knows me from the inside out, from top to bottom, and from beginning to end.

I know what it means to call my daughter mine, not in a possessive, domineering sense, but in a way that I pray secures her identity, strengthens her confidence and frees her to become a mature adult—a God-centered woman. How much more effective is God's parental love because it is love untainted by selfish motives, foolish fears and ignorance? The Lord God knows us from the inside out, from top to bottom, and from beginning to end.

> For you created my inmost being;
>> you knit me together in my mother's womb.
> I praise you because I am fearfully and wonderfully made;
>> your works are wonderful,
>> I know that full well.
> My frame was not hidden from you
>> when I was made in the secret place.
> When I was woven together in the depths of the earth,
>> your eyes saw my unformed body.
> All the days ordained for me
>> were written in your book
>> before one of them came to be. (139:13–16)

In spite of my many weaknesses, Kennerly is happy to have me as her father—at least most of the time! She does not resent that her father is older and wiser than she is (I may not always be wiser, but I will always be older). Convinced of my love, she seeks my wisdom, considers my counsel and listens to my advice. How much more, then, should I be impressed by the wisdom and counsel of God, my Maker and Redeemer?

> How precious to me are your thoughts, God!
> How vast is the sum of them!
> Were I to count them,
> They would outnumber the grains of sand—
>> when I awake, I am still with you. (139:17–18)

Who could put a price tag on the father/daughter relationship? I suppose you could add up the price of college tuition and a wedding, but like the MasterCard commercial, the relationship is "Priceless!" David is not about to do the math. How could he ever add up the thoughts of God?! The intimacy and comprehensiveness of God's love and knowledge emphasize that God is the ultimate knower.

TO KNOW IS TO BE KNOWN

British biologist Richard Dawkins vehemently objects to the notion that an all-knowing God exists. He claims, in *The God Delusion*, that any entity capable of intelligently designing something as complicated as the universe would itself have to be designed. He contends that in order for the "God Hypothesis" to be true we would have to be able to explain the existence of God. Dawkins argues that the big challenge for those who believe in God is this:

> How do they cope with the argument that any God capable of designing a universe, carefully and foresightfully tuned to lead to our evolution, must be a supremely complex and improbable entity who needs an even bigger explanation than the one he is supposed to provide?[3]

Dawkins does not want to face the daunting fact that a "who" may be responsible for the "how," that a knower may come before knowledge, a designer before the design. Although nature may have the appearance of design, Dawkins contends that to attribute nature's complexity to an intelligent designer merely removes the origin of complexity to the unseen designer. When Dawkins asks, "Who designs the designer?" he thinks he has posed the ultimate conundrum.[4] Since we can never prove God nor explain the origins of God, according to Dawkins, we can never make a convincing case for God. But if God were subject to human proofs, God would not be God.

Dawkins finds it more probable to believe that there is intelligent life elsewhere in the cosmos than to believe in the God who created the universe. He argues that "luck" and the development of life by natural selection are better explanations for life than God.

Evolution by natural selection is a brilliant answer to the riddle of the complexity because it is not a theory of chance. It is a theory of gradual, incremental change over millions of years, which starts with something very simple and works up along slow, gradual gradients to greater complexity. Not only is it a brilliant solution to the riddle of complexity; it is the only solution that has been proposed.[5]

Dawkins admits that macro-evolution may be one of the most counter-intuitive ideas ever known. He calls it the "ultimate scientific consciousness-raiser."[6] The concept of "stunning simplicity" counters one of the oldest ideas we have. Dawkins quotes Daniel Dennett to make his point, "the idea that it takes a big fancy smart thing to make a lesser thing. I call that the trickle-down theory of creation. You'll never see a spear making a spear-maker. You'll never see a horseshoe making a blacksmith. You'll never see a pot making a potter. Darwin's discovery of a workable process that does that very counter-intuitive thing is what makes his contribution to human thought so revolutionary, and so loaded with the power to raise consciousness."[7]

The problem is that science is not finding very much that is simple. We know we cannot equate simplicity with smallness. The complexity of the cosmos corresponds to the complexity of the cell. Biochemistry has revealed in the cell a miniature cosmos. Cells are not simple blobs but amazingly complex systems, made up of atoms which have their own "internal universe." If science teaches us anything, it teaches us that we cannot judge things by appearances. The table looks solid, but the physicist informs us that atoms are made up mainly of space. Protons, electrons and neutrons take up very little room and electrons are the fuzzy cloud around the nucleus.

The simplest of atoms, hydrogen, is first on the periodic table because it consists of a nucleus of one proton with one orbiting electron. But relative to its parts there is an enormous amount of space in the hydrogen atom. The radius of the hydrogen nucleus is about 1/50,000 of the distance between the nucleus and the electron. "This concept of atoms as mostly space is ultimately impossible to grasp."[8] The subatomic realm is impossible for physicists to observe directly—their findings are inferred from how atoms behave when they do things to atoms. German physicist Werner Heisenberg's Uncertainty Principle led to a new discipline known as quantum mechanics, which states that the uncertainty in the position of a particle, like an electron, is reciprocally related to the uncertainty in the momentum (or velocity) of the particle. That is to say, the better we know the particle's position the less information we have on its momentum. Thus, in any given instant, we cannot know both position and momentum simultaneously. There is a trade off of information. When asked how one could envision an atom, Heisenberg replied: "Don't try."[9] The nonintuitive nature of the quantum world is something that our brains do not appear to be wired to understand. We depend upon science to give us a new sense of logic in order to explore the universe, which constantly challenges our intuition of how the universe works. Remember, we used to think the earth was flat!

Science reveals much that at first may strike us as counterintuitive. How do we explain that water contracts as it gets colder until just before freezing, when it dramatically reverses course and expands? If water kept on contracting, lakes and streams would freeze solid from the bottom up, killing all aquatic life. Who would have imagined that the core of the earth is a molten mass with an estimated temperature range from 7,000°F to

13,000°F, about as hot as the sun?[10] At this moment we are rotating at hundreds of miles an hour around the earth's axis, and we're not even dizzy. If we lived on the equator we would be spinning a little over 1,000 miles an hour. People in San Diego are spinning at 860 mph, while those at the poles are going 0 mph, but we all are cruising through space at 66,000 mph.

Does this counterintuitive understanding of the macro and micro universe prepare us for cognitive nonsense or meaningful worship?

Scientists and theologians alike discover the counterintuitive nature of God's communication. Who would have guessed the specifics of God's self-revelation? The mystery of the Gospel is not unlike the mystery of the cosmos and the cell. The reality of the Incarnation and the truth of the Substitutionary Atonement are not what we expected, any more than we might have expected a million galaxies.

To say that knowledge is limited to only those facts that we can validate is to make ourselves out to be a god. Furthermore, from a naturalistic point of view we have no assurance that our cognitive faculties are reliable. Given the theory of unguided evolution and Darwinian processes, thinking itself is suspect. Who's to say what is real? Doesn't it make more sense to believe that our knowing is dependent on being known?

To subject the Creator to our limited criteria of proof and to make ourselves as the final arbitrator of truth is to insist on an ignorance far worse than a god-of-the-gaps. Harvard psychology professor Steven Pinker writes, "The theory of natural selection explains life as we find it, with all its quirks and tragedies... It doesn't pretend to solve one mystery (the origin of complex life) by slipping in another (the origin of a complex designer)."[11] But then, isn't that the whole point? The reality and mystery of complex life points directly—empirically—to a complex design and to a creator. Note that I say it "points" to a creator. I'm not claiming it scientifically proves a creator. There is evidence to the contrary. In a number of phenomena, including a number of apparently random and violent phenomena, it is now fairly well understood that the driving processes can be childishly simple even though they produce extremely complex end states. In these cases, complexity comes from simplicity. The point being made here does not rest on making the case that all natural phenomena moves from complexity to complexity. The point is that it is not unreasonable to observe natural phenomena and come to the conclusion that life did not just happen—the random product of time and chance. Nothing is being slipped in surreptitiously. It is there for all to see—the undeniable truth that cannot be ignored, unless of course one insists on ignoring the evidence (Psalm 14:1). This is not merely a devotional truth that only pertains to an existential point-of-view, but the very truth that is foundational to doing science and keeping one's sanity.

Dawkins concludes that science puts "us in our place...scaling down our vanity to fit the tiny stage on which we play out our lives—our speck of debris from the cosmic explosion."[12] What I find so amazing is that Dawkins can get away with saying the earth, relative to the cosmos, is nothing more than a speck of debris, and that life evolves from the simple to the complex, like a horseshoe making a blacksmith! Is this hubris masquerading as humility or brilliance grasping the counterintuitive essence of science?

If knowledge is ultimately personal—rooted in relationships rather than in impersonal data, then faith, hope and love are essential to knowing—not just feeling, but *knowing*. We may know the facts about someone but that doesn't mean we know them. We may even know personal details about their life, but without knowing the person we don't really know them. Doesn't it seem strange that what we find commonplace in interpersonal relationships is so easily dismissed as myth-making and make-believe when it comes to knowing God? Why is it so hard to believe that the vast amounts of information in the universe are intentionally designed to reveal, inform and even inspire? Which came first, the knower or knowledge, the informer or information, the designer or design? "For the Christian, the efficacy of one's faith lies not in faith itself but in the faithfulness of the One who is the object of that faith. In other words, our faith is only as good as the One we're trusting. If God is not faithful to his Word, then our faith can accomplish nothing at all."[13]

DO WE LIVE IN A MORAL UNIVERSE?

The psalmist is appropriately humbled by God's intimate understanding of himself, and cannot begin to match his knowledge with God's. The psalm highlights four responses to the all-knowing, inescapable God. Being known inspires awe and worship, a profound sense of providential security, a passionate commitment to God in the real life spiritual battle, and the truest form of vulnerability, divine self-examination. "Search me, God, and know my heart."

When my daughter was young, she looked to me to protect and defend her, and I enjoyed being my daughter's advocate, guardian and defender. I still do, but soon we'll be reversing roles. Just as a child turns to a loving parent, we turn to our heavenly Father. This relationship did not create our understanding of God. On the contrary, our relationship with God creates the parent-child relationship. If I am a true dad, my daughter will be free to come to me and vent her feelings and frustrations, her anger and her pain. As David turned to God and vented his hatred of evil, we learn to pour out our anger and despair to God.

> If only you would slay the wicked, O God!
>   Away from me, you who are bloodthirsty!
> They speak of you with evil intent;
>   your adversaries misuse your name.
> Do I not hate those who hate you, Lord,
>   and abhor those who are in rebellion against you?
> I have nothing but hatred for them;
>   I count them my enemies. (Psalm 139:19–22)

When we read the ending to Psalm 139, our first inclination is to perform a "psalmectomy." We want to edit these harsh sounding words, but how can we and remain faithful to a moral universe? Is moral pain real or a figment of our imagination? The question of knowing and being known always seems to raise moral questions. Who invented right and wrong? According to Richard Dawkins, no one. Dawkins contends that good and evil do not exist: "Nature is not cruel, only pitilessly indifferent. This is one of the hardest lessons for humans to learn. We cannot admit that things might be neither good nor evil, neither cruel nor kind, but simply callous—indifferent to all suffering, lacking all purpose."[14] This is why we need to bring the truth of this psalm into the physics classroom if we expect to do science with any sense of personal knowing and moral order.

When Dr. Francis Collins, head of the Human Genome Project, was in his twenties, he began to question his confident atheism. After reading the first chapter in *Mere Christianity* by C. S. Lewis, entitled, "Right and Wrong as a Clue to the Meaning of the Universe," Collins felt the bright white light of the Moral Law shining into the recesses of his "childish atheism."[15] The fact that Collins could not explain away the law of human nature as a cultural artifact or evolutionary by-product rocked his ideas about science and spirit right down to their foundation.[16] Human beings appear to have a universal sense of right and wrong. Is this an intrinsic quality for humans or a consequence of cultural traditions? Collins wrestled with this question and came to the conclusion that the best explanation for the moral law was a Moral Law Giver. Collins explains,

> The hardwired behavior of the worker ant is thus fundamentally different from the inner voice that causes me to feel compelled to jump into the river to try to save a drowning stranger, even if I'm not a good swimmer and may myself die in the effort.

"If God exists," thought Collins, "then He must be outside the natural world, and therefore the tools of science are not the right ones to learn about Him. Instead, as I was beginning to understand from looking into my own heart, the evidence of God's existence would have to come from other directions, and the ultimate decision would be based on faith, not proof."[17]

David ends the psalm by inviting the Lord to examine his heart and expose his sin. More than anything else he is glad to be fully known by his God. He is well aware that nothing escapes God's notice. His thoughts and feelings are an open book before him. In fact, everything about him, past, present and future, is completely comprehended by God. Finally the psalmist personally invites God's scrutiny and testing.

> Search me, God, and know my heart;
> test me and know my anxious thoughts.

See if there is any offensive way in me,
and lead me in the way everlasting. (139:23–24)

We worship God for who he is and what he has done, but in worship we also discover who we are and what we have done. Worship tells the truth about God, but it also confronts us with the truth about ourselves. Convinced of God's love and holiness, his sovereign wisdom and enduring comfort, David invites divine examination. Are we willing to say to the Lord what David said? "See if there is any offensive way in me."

THINK SACRAMENTALLY

In his address to the intellectual elite in Athens, Paul applied the wisdom of Psalm 139. He spoke of the immediacy of God's sovereign presence and the power of God over all creation and history. His main thrust was to make a case for the independence of God and the dependence of all human beings on the God of Creation. Paul believed that the truth of God could be inferred from what God had made. "For since the creation of the world God's invisible qualities—his eternal power and divine nature—have been clearly seen, being understood from what has been made, so that people are without excuse" (Romans 1:20). Scientists speak of atoms as if they could clearly see them, even though they can only infer their existence from their effect. Paul spoke in a similar way of God.

In Athens, Paul refuted idol-ignorance with Logos-logic. He described an idol as "an image made by human design and skill" that substitutes for God. Idols can be either metal objects or mental constructs. Images sculpted in exquisite detail are no more or less idolatrous than mental concepts which contend that the earth is a speck of cosmic debris. The Hebrew prophets mocked the logic of people who put their hope in inanimate statutes of wood and gold. Is ancient idolatry any more illogical than the modern idolatry that asserts that the potter was made by the pot and the blacksmith was made by the horseshoe?

Paul's audience on Mars Hill suffered from a case of sophisticated ignorance, not unlike people today who insist on nature alone. Paul used their idol to the Unknown God to make known to the Athenians their ignorance of the nature of God and his justice. They were ignorant of God's intervention in creation through salvation history, and they were ignorant of the man appointed by God to bring about justice and judgment. Paul brought his message home by refuting idolatry, calling for repentance and warning of a set time of judgment. "In the past God overlooked such ignorance, but now he commands all people everywhere to repent. For he has set a day when he will judge the world with justice by the man he has appointed. He has given *proof* of this to everyone by raising him from the dead" (Acts 17:31).

The "proof" that Paul had in mind is not a scientific proof, the kind that can be replicated in the laboratory through repeatable experiments. He meant a more relational confirmation based on trust and a shared understanding of God's acts in history. This evidence consists of the relational bond that exists between God and his creation. This "proof" lies outside of science but it is for science. It is in history, but not explainable by historical forces. This proof is not on the order of a contract, but a covenant. Paul uses the resurrection of Jesus Christ as the ultimate relational proof to verify God's intentions for creation and humanity. The resurrection is an historical event that proves God's faithfulness to his Word. The resurrection validates and verifies that life is meaningful and that meaning itself is rooted in the ultimate Knower. Paul's Athenian discourse affirms the sacramental vision of life. All of life is sacred because everything was intended to be related to its Creator and Redeemer.

> The 'sacramental vision' is a vision of the interconnectedness of all discrete elements of human experience and physical reality such that the world appears as one vast and coherent whole; a satisfying vision of the mysterious and meaningful significances attached to all facets of life, even the mundane and the ordinary.[18]

Psalm 139 is filled with first-person personal pronouns: *I, me* and *my.* The emphasis, however, is not on the self, but on the Lord. The best way to avoid self-centeredness, as David knew so well, is not by pretending that the self does not exist, or by self-consciously trying to eliminate all personal references. To be truly God-centered is a deeply personal experience. Instead of living according to the constant refrain "Me! Me! Me!" we enter into a hymn of praise and adoration: "Holy, holy, holy is the Lord God Almighty, who was, and is, and is to come" (Revelation 4:8). Everything about me becomes centered in the Lord Jesus Christ, my abilities and disabilities, my hopes and fears, my friends and enemies, my past and future, my daily tasks and long-range goals.

Faith implies humility, "Now I know in part" (knowledge is both limited and dependent). Hope inspires confidence, "then I shall know fully" (knowledge is destined for fulfillment not frustration). Love insists on relationship, "even as I am fully known," (knowledge is personal and complete). "And now these three remain: faith, hope and love. But the greatest of these is love" (1 Corinthians 13:12–13).

4

THE LANGUAGE OF GOD

"Were not our hearts burning within us while he talked
with us on the road and opened the Scriptures to us?"

Luke 24:32

Some time ago a full page ad on the back cover of *Christianity Today* pictured a line of satellite dishes pointing out to space. The caption read, "I wish God wanted to talk to me half as much as I wanted to hear from Him." Many people, Christians included, seem to think that God could do a better job staying in touch. The famous English mathematician and atheist Bertrand Russell (author of *Why I Am Not a Christian*) was reportedly asked on his deathbed what he would say if he discovered that in fact there was a God. He replied, "I think I should say to him: Sir, it appears that my atheistic hypothesis was erroneous. Would you mind answering me one little question? Why didn't you give us more evidence? Not enough evidence, God, not enough evidence."[1]

Far from being disappointed with God's ability to communicate, David was awed by the evidence for God, both in the world and in his own nature. Instead of ingratiating himself to his readers by lamenting that God had not fulfilled their expectations, David celebrated the power and effectiveness of God's language to communicate.

Psalm 19 is as fine a representation of the psalms as we could imagine. This hymn of praise to God celebrates the testimony of God in creation and the revelation of God through His word. And it does this in a way that reflects the creativity and wonder of creation. We don't know the ancient Hebrew melody of David's prayer, but we can imagine the power of this testimony when we hear Haydn's setting of Psalm 19 in *The Creation*.

We find a power in the clarity and beauty of this psalm that is sufficient to silence the otherwise deafening noise of the information age. Against the din of crunching data and the sensory overload of special effects, we are called to listen to primary communication—the language of our mother tongue. The heavens declare the glory of God; the skies proclaim the work of his hands. A single message is prayed out in parallel lines, each reinforcing the other and made more vivid with meaningful metaphors. One short poetic prayer to the Lord as Creator and Moral Law Giver refutes the world's materialism and relativism and leads us in worship.

If all that mattered was processing biblical information, the psalms would never have been written. Their poetic power and creative beauty is in keeping with the truth they convey. The psalms are alive and dynamic, informing the mind and inspiring the heart; bearing witness and guiding worship. The truth that is most central to our being transcends equations and data processing, but delights the soul. Each new day reminds the worshiper of a bridegroom's joy or marathoner's race to the finish. Creation is alive with passion and joy.

The Spirit-inspired psalmist is fully attentive and listening intently to the message of God. David is all ears to what God has to say. The silent testimony of God is spoken everywhere. The message is not whispered, it is *declared*. It is a universal language that knows no bounds. "There is no speech or language where their voice is not heard. Their voice goes out into all the earth, their words to the ends of the world." This is why the apostle Paul wrote,

> For since the creation of the world God's invisible qualities—his eternal power and divine nature—have been clearly seen, being understood from what has been made, so that people are without excuse (Romans 1:20).

Can it be said that the language of God is our mother tongue? We were meant to resonate with God's speech personally. It is in the character of our souls to want to hear truth and to be true. The Author of Life, whose speech creates and sustains the universe, has endowed us with this built-in longing. As Augustine said, our hearts are restless until they find their rest in God. Richard Baxter, the seventeenth-century advocate for pastoral reform, compared people to "broken syllables" apart from the Author of Life.

> We know little of the creature, till we know it as it stands related to the Creator: single letters, and syllables uncomposed, are no better than nonsense. He who overlooks him who is the 'Alpha and Omega, the beginning and the end,' and sees not him in all who is the All of all, does see nothing at all. All creatures, as such are broken syllables; they signify nothing as separated from God.[2]

Years ago, while teaching in Toronto, I met a missionary in one of my seminary classes who had just returned from a four year term in France with his wife and children. They had spent most of their first term trying to learn the language. The experience became needlessly and regretfully traumatic. When they arrived in France, he vowed he would only use French and not speak a word of English to his wife and children. The effect of the vow was disastrous. His version of devotion and zeal created unnecessary strains in the marriage and a negative impact on his children. When they returned to Canada they all found it very difficult to speak in English. It is unnatural for anyone to forget their native language—their mother tongue. Many of us spend so much time speaking the language of the world that we forget the Word of God. It is as if we have vowed to speak only the language of Babel.

When Jesus entered Jerusalem on the Sunday before the crucifixion, the crowds were shouting "Hosanna!" They were saying, "Blessed is the king who comes in the name of the Lord!" and "Peace in heaven and glory in the highest!" Some of the Pharisees took offense and said to Jesus, "Teacher, rebuke your disciples!" Jesus replied, "I tell you if they keep quiet, the stones will cry out" (Luke 19:38–40).

A marine biologist can pick up a seashell and, through careful listening, learn much about what happened in the lifetime of its inhabitant and in the evolution of its species. Every geologist knows that even the rocks speak, telling tales across gaps of time far wider than recorded history, stories we would not know if human vocalization were the only speech we could hear. Annie Dillard titled one of her books *Teaching a Stone to Talk*, but the real issue, as Dillard knows, is teaching ourselves to listen. The inner life of any great thing will be incomprehensible to me until I develop and deepen an inner life of my own. I cannot know in another being what I do not know in myself.[3]

EARS TO HEAR

Jesus often left the crowd with the refrain, "He who has ears to hear let him hear." As if to say, "The message is clear, it's up to you whether you take it in." In Genesis, the line, "And God said, `Let there be...'", is repeated nine times for emphasis. Everything is responsive to the Word of God. This makes it all the more ironic that the unmistakable voice of our Creator should fall on deaf ears.

In Carl Sagan's novel, *Contact*, radio astronomers are involved in a search for extra-terrestrial intelligence (SETI). They monitor millions of radio signals from outer space in the hopes of picking up an intelligible signal from a distant planet. Among the myriad of naturally produced random radio signals (e.g. pulsars) the SETI researchers listen for a sound pattern that would indicate that there is intelligible life on another planet. In real life no such radio signal has ever been detected, but in the novel the astronomers pick up a signal that does not appear to be random. It is a sequence of 1126 bits representing prime numbers from 2 to 101. The complexity and specificity of the signal pattern implies that someone has designed a message. As one SETI researcher said, "This isn't noise, this has structure."

The novel reflects the late Carl Sagan's optimism that in the not too distant future we will make contact with extra-terrestrial intelligence. It also implies his confidence in distinguishing between that which is random and that which infers design. Because of the complexity and specificity of the radio signal, scientists naturally concluded that the signal was intentional. Carl Sagan was prepared to accept the inference of design and

SECOND THOUGHTS FOR SKEPTICS

agency from extra-terrestrial beings, but adamant in his refusal to accept evidence for creation and design in this world. He'd rather trust in an interplanetary bar code than the revelation of God in nature.

For decades, scientists raised on Darwinian assumptions have assumed "that the world can be rationally comprehensible only if it is entirely the product of irrational, unguided mechanisms." Phillip Johnson continues, "On the contrary, the rationality and reliability of the scientific mind rests on the fact that the mind was designed in the image of the mind of the creator, who made both the laws and our capacity to understand them."[4]

Leading scientists, steeped in philosophical materialism, are opposed to design. Richard Dawkins begins his book, *The Blind Watchmaker*, by stating, "Biology is the study of complicated things that give the appearance of having been designed for a purpose." Francis Crick, Nobel laureate and co-discoverer of the structure of DNA, writes, "Biologists must constantly keep in mind that what they see was not designed, but rather evolved."[5]

David was confident in the clarity and universality of the testimony of creation. "Day after day they pour forth speech; night after night they display knowledge." For those who hear *the heavens declare the glory of God*, the message comes through loud and clear, but for the materialist, it comes through as gibberish. I cannot understand a person who is speaking Mandarin, but that doesn't give me the right to conclude that his or her language is unintelligible. My inability to distinguish noise from speech in no way diminishes the Chinese language. Scientists who are committed to an impersonal, irrational interpretation of the universe, regardless of what the evidence reveals, will never hear the heavens declaring the glory of God.

THE LANGUAGES OF GOD

The human capacity for language sets us apart in creation. "We are the only creatures in this incredible, vast creation, that deal with language," writes Eugene Peterson:

> Language is unique to us human beings. Turnips complete a fairly complex and useful life cycle without the use of words. Roses grace the world with extraordinary beauty and fragrance without uttering a word.. . . It is quite impressive really, what goes on around us without words: ocean tides, mountain heights, stormy weather, turning constellations, genetic codes, bird migrations—most, in fact, of what we see and hear around us, a great deal of it incredibly complex, but without language, wordless. And we, we human beings, have words. We can use language. We are the only ones in this stunning kaleidoscopic array of geology and biology and astronomy, to use words.
>
> We share a great deal with the rest of creation. We have much in common with everything around us, the dirt beneath our feet, the animals around us, the stars above us, and we recognize links in this family identity. But when it comes down to understanding our humanity, who we are in this vast scheme of things, we find ourselves attending to language, the fact that we speak words, and what happens to us when we do. . . . The one who reveals God to us is named Word. This human nature of ours with its mysterious and unique capacity for language is paralleled in the nature of God. God speaks. In the term we use to refer to our interest in God, theology, the two words are set along side each other and then combined; *theo* meaning God and *logos* meaning word. *Theos* is capable of *logos*, logos is characteristic of *theos*. Then the significance of this parallel hits us: We are capable of speech; God reveals himself in speech. In the complete revelation of God, the Word became flesh.[6]

The psalmist uses the human capacity for intelligible words and thoughts to speak of the other languages of God: "They have no speech, they use no words; no sound is heard from them. Yet their voice goes out into all the earth, their words to the ends of the world" (Psalm 19:3–4).

THE LANGUAGE OF MOLECULAR BIOLOGY

On June 26, 2000, it was announced at the White House that the first draft of the human genome had been assembled. President Clinton said on that occasion, "Today we are learning the language in which God created life. We are gaining ever more awe for the complexity, the beauty, and the wonder of God's most divine and sacred gift." Francis Collins who headed up the Human Genome Project resonated with the President's speech. He wrote, "For me the experience of sequencing the human genome, and uncovering this most remarkable of all texts, was both a stunning scientific achievement and an occasion of worship." Collins calls the human genome "the language of God" because it lays out in a readable form "the intimate details of how humans came to be."[7]

What is especially remarkable and should not be taken for granted is that humans can read this particular revelation of the language of God. Living organisms bear a remarkable similarity when it comes to gene count, but "no other organism has sequenced its own genome."[8]

For years molecular biologists believed in a theory they called the "central dogma." Barry Commoner, senior scientist at the Center for Biology of Natural Systems at Queen's College, City University of New York, explains, "The premise assumes that an organism's genome—its total complement of DNA genes—should fully account for its characteristic assemblage of inherited traits."[9] Originally, it was thought that there was a gene for every inherited trait. Thus, if the entire human genome was mapped out, the ability to safely modify defective genes or even alter selective genes would be doable. Thanks to the Human Genome Project we now know it is much more complicated than that. To their surprise, scientists learned that there are only about 20,000–25,000 protein-coding genes in the human genome, when they expected to find at least 100,000.

Gene counts for organisms such as worms, flies, and simple plants seem to be about the same as humans, around 20,000— "hardly an adequate basis for distinguishing among 'life as a fly, a carrot, or a man.'"[10] Within the human species, "at the DNA level, we are all 99.9 percent identical."[11] As it turns out, "there is much more to the "ultimate description of life" than our genes, on their own can tell us."[12] "We are all 99.9 percent the same, but equally, in the words of the biochemist David Cox, 'you could say all humans share nothing, and that would be correct, too.'"[13]

Scientists now recognize genes as letters in an alphabet that can be arranged in all sorts of ways. If the twenty-six letters in the English alphabet can produce an estimated one to two million words, just think of the endless variety possible with more than 20,000 genes. Science writer Bill Bryson likens genes to keys on a piano, "each playing a single note and nothing else, which is obviously a trifle monotonous. But combine the genes, as you would combine piano keys, and you can create chords and melodies of infinite variety. Put all these genes together, and you have (to continue the metaphor) the great symphony of existence known as the human genome."[14]

However, it is much more complicated than any analogy is able to suggest. Each of us has about six feet of DNA squeezed into almost every cell. "Each length of DNA comprises some 3.2 billion letters of coding, enough to provide 10 to 3,480,000,000 possible combinations."[15] However, most of our DNA, like ninety-seven percent "consists of nothing but long stretches of meaningless garble—'junk,' or non-coding DNA, as biochemists prefer to put it. Only here and there along each strand do you find sections that control and organize vital functions. These are curious and long-elusive genes."[16]

> The molecular events that accomplish this genetic reshuffling are focused on a particular stage in the overall DNA–RNA–protein, progression. It occurs when the DNA gene's nucleotide sequence is transferred to the next genetic carrier—messenger RNA. A specialized group of fifty to sixty proteins, together with five small molecules of RNA—known as a 'spliceosome'—assembles at sites along the length of the messenger RNA, where it cuts apart various segments of the messenger RNA. Certain of these fragments are spliced together into a number of alternative combinations, which then have nucleotide sequences that differ from the gene's original one. These numerous, redesigned messenger RNAs govern the production of an equal number of proteins that differ in their amino acid sequence and hence in the inherited traits that they engender. For example, when the word TIME is rearranged to read MITE, EMIT, and ITEM, three alternative units of information are created from an original one.[17]

In other words, Francis Crick's "central dogma" that once genetic information passed into protein it could not get out again was wrong. The whole process of genetic sequencing is immensely more complicated than first proposed, proving as well that genetic engineering is more dangerous than we might have thought. However, it is not just the complexity of sequencing that should impress us, but the very nature of molecular communication. There is a kind of mind over matter quality to everything that goes on in life. Everything in biochemistry is so information rich. There is nothing "dumbed down" about the universe. Not only is the "central dogma" exposed as myth—the simple idea of a one-for-one correspondence between gene and inherited trait, but there appears to be no simplicity on this side of complexity. The macro-evolutionary dogma that contends life moved from simple organism to complex organism is as mythical as the thesis of "irreducible complexity." Whether we are examining the cosmos or the "inner universe" of the cell, we find an immense, overwhelming complexity.

In making a case for a moral universe, Lewis writes, "You can hardly imagine a bit of matter giving instructions."[18] But that's exactly what matter does. Cells are constantly communicating, and they are telling us what we are made of, but not how we work. The next step for science is to crack the human proteome—the library of information that creates proteins— but each discovery opens up a new vista that takes us deeper into the mystery and complexity of life. The more we learn how creation communicates, the more we can appreciate by faith the fact that the universe is sustained by the Word of God. As the author of Hebrews says, "The Son is the radiance of God's glory and the exact representation of his being, sustaining all things by his powerful word" (Hebrews 1:3).

THE LANGUAGE OF MATHEMATICS

Albert Einstein said, "The most incomprehensible thing about the universe is that it is comprehensible." That would be true, but only if you attributed the origin of life to luck and the development of nature to a purposeless process of natural selection. If on the other hand, life is infused with meaning in every sphere and from every angle, then the intelligibility of the universe from top to bottom is understandable and really not very surprising at all. The famous Hungarian physicist and mathematician E. P. Wigner wrote about *The Unreasonable Effectiveness of Mathematics in the Natural Sciences*:

> The enormous usefulness of mathematics in the natural sciences is something bordering on the mysterious. . . .There is no rational explanation for it. . .The miracle of the appropriateness of the language of mathematics for the formulation of the laws of physics is a wonderful gift which we neither understand nor deserve.[19]

We are not born knowing arithmetic, algebra, calculus or geometry. This knowledge is acquired, not for utilitarian purposes alone, but for the formal beauty that drives mathematical development.[20] Mathematics is a science of discovery on the order of molecular biology, driven by "the mathematician's desire for formal beauty" and a quest for absolute answers. Math is an acquired language of order and beauty that has evolved in silent defiance of Darwin's theory of natural selection. That it should illuminate the order of nature with such precision is baffling from the standpoint of biological reductionism, but completely consistent with an intelligible universe. As any physicist will tell you, studying nature without mathematics would be like calling a baseball game without using numbers. Astronomer Sir James Jeans proclaimed, "God is a pure mathematician."[21] The mathematical nature of the universe from beehives to butterfly wings is truly overwhelming.

My father was a math professor at a community college teaching calculus and other inscrutable mysteries. I didn't have a clue as to the kind of math my father was working so hard on. He could spend days working on a single math problem. The only time we talked about math was when I came to him with a homework math problem that I couldn't figure out. All I wanted was the right answer, but my father was intent on explaining to me how the math worked. He wanted me to grasp the beauty of mathematics—to learn the language.

Mathematics is not the language of God because it reveals secret codes, although plenty of people have tried to use numbers that way. There may be some uncanny coincidences when it comes to numbers, but mathematics, pure and simple and secular, speaks of a reasoned universe with geometric beauty, specific precision, and absolute answers. Math "directs the imagination towards an apprehension of totality."[22] When we have numbered something, devised an equation, mapped a distance, measured the volume, and analyzed discrete units, we feel we have come closer to touching reality and accounting for it. The word of the psalmist, "Teach us to number our days, that we may gain a heart of wisdom," can be applied in many ways (Psalm 90:12).

THE LANGUAGE OF MUSIC

We know the difference between random sounds that make noise and music that moves the soul. "It is no secret to most of us," writes Thomas Dubay, "that great music can stir and move, soothe and comfort, inflame and enkindle, enthuse and inspire, evoke and elicit, uplift and stimulate, thrill and transport, sparkle and refresh, grip and enthrall, touch one's heartstrings and draw tears, enlighten and touch."[23] How can notes on a score played by a musician with mathematical precision and artistic passion move people in such a powerful way? How can music be so intangible, yet so real? Shakespeare's character Benedick in *Much Ado about Nothing*, asks, "Is it not strange that sheep's gut should hale souls out of men's bodies?"[24]

Music has been called the universal language because of its ability to transcend cultural barriers. Michael Platt says, "Music is unique among human pursuits in being able to overcome the vast gulf between rare virtue and common aptitude. It is the most mathematical of the fine arts. It is science and fun together."[25]

Suppose someone with a reductionistic bent were to review one of Mozart's symphonies:

> We have been able to prove that this particular symphony is actually reducible to a series of notes that happen to be played both at the same time in chords and one after another, creating a string of disturbances in the air caused by different frequencies. We realize, of course, that those disturbances cause further disturbances in the audience, due in part to the presence of Earth's particular atmosphere and in part to the effect such disturbances have on the apparatus of the ear as transmitted by neurons to the brain—so disturbing, in fact, that some break into involuntary tears, remarking that they seemed to be hearing the very harmonies of heaven. Happily, we now know that there is nothing more to Mozart's work in particular and to music in general than mere notes, themselves reducible to waves disturbing the air.[26]

Richard Dawkins argues that "Schubert's musical brain is a wonder of improbability, even more so than the vertebrate's eye."[27] According to Dawkins the reason we have such sublime art is because it was sponsored by the enormous wealth of the church. Artists had to earn a living and the church was paying the bills. "How sad," Dawkins writes, "that we shall never hear Beethoven's *Mesozoic Symphony*, or Mozart's opera *The Expanding Universe*. And what shame that we are deprived of Haydn's *Evolution Oratorio*—but that does not stop us from enjoying his *Creation*."[28] For Dawkins, great music is the product of sponsorship rather than the inspiration of God. The argument for the existence of God from beauty does not impress him. It angers him.

We have all experienced the power of music to speak to the soul. Kent Nerburn describes his reaction to Leonard Bernstein conducting Beethoven's Ninth in a concert that celebrated the fall of the Berlin Wall:

> The instruments sang as if with one voice. The music rose and expanded and became pure emotion. Tears streamed from my eyes. . . . .It was more than I was, and more than I could be. It was a healing and a testament to the best of who we are and the worst of who we are. It was confession, it was celebration. It was us at our most human. By the time the concert was over, I had been transformed. Into my daily life had come a moment of sheer beauty.[29]

The "voices" of molecular biology, mathematics, and music, to name only three, *declare*, in their own special way, "the glory of God." "Day after day they pour forth speech; night after night they display knowledge." Lewis warns us to be careful and not mistake the medium for the message. Like an infatuated lover, who has fallen in love with the feeling of love, rather than with the true object of his devotion, we are in danger of falling in love with molecules or math or music, and missing the message.

> The books or the music in which we thought the beauty was located will betray us if we trust in them; it was not *in* them, it only came *through* them, and what came through them was longing. . . . For they are not the thing itself; they are only the scent of a flower we have not found, the echo of a tune we have not heard, news from a country we have not yet visited.[30]

THE MORAL LANGUAGE

The psalmist transitions from the eloquence of God's continuous, abundant, and universal revelation in creation to the Lord's explicit guidance and instruction in the Law. For the psalmist, the molecular universe and the moral universe are one. The laws of nature and moral law make up an integrated whole that cannot be compartmentalized. In the first six verses, the name of God is used only once and it is the least specific name for God in the Bible (*El*, Psalm 19:1). But in the next stanza, the personal name of God, Yahweh (the Lord), is heard seven times. The wisdom of God which has been inferred from the beauty and complexity of creation is now made explicit in the statutes, precepts, commands, and ordinances of the Lord. Knowing how to live in God's creation is not left to fate. The Lord gives precise and authoritative guidance. As the apostle Paul wrote, "All Scripture is God-breathed and is useful for teaching, rebuking, correcting and training in righteousness, so that the person of God may be thoroughly equipped for every good work" (2 Timothy 3:16).

The complexity of creation and the specificity of biblical revelation is not an accident. There is a moral and spiritual counterpart to the wonderful beauty of nature. The impressive order and design of the physical universe parallels the order and structure designed for human relationships. In both spheres there is precision and authority. These statutes, laws, precepts, and commandments may sound burdensome to those who do not understand that the moral order is also finely tuned and a reflection of the character of God. We need this wisdom, and the Lord's guidance is altogether positive, reviving the soul, making wise the simple, and giving joy to the heart. The purpose of revelation is not to fill our lives with information, but "to bring God's will to bear on [us] and evoke intelligent reverence, well-founded trust, detailed obedience."[31]

SPEAKING OUR LANGUAGE

If we have ears to hear the testimony of creation and the wisdom of revelation, then what follows next in this psalm will strike us as both natural and necessary. How can we hear the heavens declare the glory of God and heed the warning of the commands of God without humbly praying for forgiveness of our hidden faults and deliverance from our wilful sins? "The psalmist moves in a climactic fashion from macrocosm to microcosm, from the universe and its glory to the individual in humility before God."[32]

The last line of the psalm, "O, Lord, my Rock and my Redeemer," causes us to think of our Lord and Savior, Jesus Christ. The Incarnation of God adds a third climactic movement to the revelation of God. "The Word became flesh and made his dwelling among us. We have seen his glory, the glory of the One and Only, who came from the Father, full of grace and truth" (John 1:14). The One in whom are hidden all the treasures of wisdom and knowledge (Colossians 2:3) fulfills the testimony of creation and the commands of revelation with the gospel of redemption.

As we confess our sins and pray for deliverance, we join with creation in declaring the glory of God and we affirm the wisdom of the Lord. Only those who listen well to the testimony of God are the ones who truly pray this prayer: "May the words of my mouth and the meditation of my heart be pleasing in your sight, O Lord, my Rock and my Redeemer." By the Spirit of Christ we follow-up the witness of creation and revelation. The words of our mouth and the meditations of our heart declare the glory, affirm the precepts, and share the good news of Jesus Christ, our Rock and our Redeemer.

A RESURRECTION CONVERSATION

The question of meaning eventually comes around to the reality of the resurrection. Paul claimed you can't have the one without the other. "If only for this life we have hope in Christ, we are to be pitied more than all others" (1 Corinthians 15:19). The *glory*, as in the "heavens declare the glory of God" assumes a specificity and preciseness that defies generalizations and impersonal abstractions. The ordinary is not so ordinary. The mundane world of cells and stars, notes and numbers, proves far more momentous than we ever imagined. Everything borders on the incomprehensible, nothing is simple. The frontiers of knowledge are everywhere. God is there and he is not silent, "sustaining all things by his powerful word" (Hebrews 1:3).

On the road to Emmaus, Jesus drew near to two disciples who had just come from Jerusalem. They were fresh from the tragedy of the crucifixion that had claimed the life of their prophet, friend, and hoped-for-redeemer. They were in grief, lamenting what might have been, when Jesus "came up and walked along with them; but they were kept from recognizing him" (Luke 24:15–16).

Jesus began the conversation with a question, "What are you discussing together as you walk along?" This alone is cause for amazement. Why should the risen Lord be interested in what they were talking about? Isn't this a miracle in itself? Why does God care? "What is man that you are mindful of him and the son of man that you care for him?" (Psalm 8). These two disciples were incredulous. How could anyone coming from Jerusalem be so clueless as to not know what had happened these past few days in that city. They mistook his question for ignorance and considered themselves knowledgeable. They were like the scientist or the philosopher who falsely assumes the upper hand in a dialogue without even a thought that they stand in the very presence of God.

THE LANGUAGE OF GOD

"What things?" Jesus asked. Why did the risen Lord play along? Why does God put up with our ignorance? Jesus patiently listened to them describe the events, express their hopes, and report their amazement. "But they didn't find his body," they said. Clearly, knowledge was limited to their experience, colored by their emotion, and ignorant of the one who walked with them. Like these two disciples, we tend to act as if we know the score and we're explaining things to novices. We are so ready with the explanation, so quick to speak and slow to listen. They asked incredulously, "Are you the only one in Jerusalem who hasn't heard what's happened during the last few days?"

Their perspective on these events was not as harmless and as excusable as we may think. They should have known better, just as we should know better. Jesus launched into the big picture of Salvation History. "How foolish you are, and how slow to believe all that the prophets have spoken! Did not the Messiah have to suffer these things and then enter his glory?" Luke continues, "And beginning with Moses and all the Prophets, he explained to them what was said in all the Scriptures concerning himself" (Luke 24:25–27).

His explanation of the facts preceded their recognition of him, but even before they recognized him—before he took bread, gave thanks, broke it and began to give it to them—they experienced an excitement and an intensity that they themselves could not explain away. The truth was on fire within their bones before they recognized who it was that was walking with them. "Were not our hearts burning within us while he talked with us on the road and opened the Scriptures to us?" (Luke 24:32). Explanation and experience combined to lead to recognition. The truth of the Resurrection was not only the outcome of the Emmaus road conversation, but the culmination of all true explanations and genuine experiences. All the languages of God end in an understanding of the risen Lord Jesus Christ.

> O Gracious and Holy Father,
> give us wisdom to perceive You,
> diligence to seek You, patience to wait for You,
> eyes to behold You, a heart to meditate on You,
> and a life to proclaim You;
> through the power of the Spirit of Jesus Christ our Lord

St. Benedict c. 480–547

THE SEARCH FOR MEANING

"But where can wisdom be found? Where does under-
standing dwell? No mortal comprehends its worth;
it cannot be found in the land of the living."

Job 28:12

The human exploration of nature is celebrated in the Book
of Job. In the midst of extreme suffering and alienation,
Job is compelled to reflect on the ingenuity of brave explorers
and ancient technologists. His *Ode to Science*, delivered in the
middle of his agonizing despair, serves as a unique testimony
to the human quest for meaning. Job revels in the human
pursuit of knowledge, which proves far superior to that of
any other creature. Bildad, one of Job's counselors, finishes
up his argument with a rhetorical stinger by declaring that
mere mortals are maggots—"a human being, who is only a
worm!" (Job 25:6). From a genetic perspective, Bildad has a
point, because we share about the same number of genes as an
earthworm, but Job challenges Bildad's nihilistic perspective by
celebrating human exploration, engineering, and courage. The
measure of a human being must be beyond the gene count.

FATE OR FAITH?

"Does God care?" is a question running through the entire dialogue. Job's counselors conclude that God doesn't care, but Job refuses to accept this answer. Human nature's capacity for love and reason, intelligence and creativity, situated in a universe designed for discovery, convinces Job otherwise. In frustration, Job's trio of tormenters sound increasingly fatalistic, while Job's faith in God builds in spite of his pain. He clings tenaciously to two convictions. First, he will not let go of the idea that his righteousness matters to God. He is convinced that his refusal to disobey God and admit to a wrong he did not do, means something to God. And second, he believes in a physical and moral universe created by God. Life is endowed with a purpose and meaning given to it by a just and sovereign God.

Job's "friends" are more in line with the ancient Greek philosopher Epicurus (ca 342–270 BC), who reasoned that the universe was accidental, the random collision and adhesion of matter, and that humans were just one of an infinite number of accidents. When, eighteen centuries later, Copernicus discovered that the Earth was not the center of the cosmos, he seemed to confirm the *disanthropic* nature of the universe. The cosmos is not human centered after all. The Sun does not revolve around the Earth, and our little planet looks relatively pointless in the grand scheme of the millions of galaxies. This fueled the notion among many scientists that there must be intelligent life somewhere else in the universe. Disanthropism fits those who argue that the origin of life was a matter of sheer luck.

If the Copernican revolution seemed to scale back Earth's special significance, the anthropic principle has not only restored it, but has increased it. Science has discovered a host of precise mathematical regularities that are essential for complex carbon-based intelligent life to exist. The anthropic principle refers to the more than two dozen parameters for the universe that must have values falling within narrowly defined ranges for life of any kind to exist.[1] A "just right" universe involves a precision balance of electromagnetism, strong and weak nuclear forces, gravitational forces, ratios of electron to proton mass and protons to electrons. The universe, its expansion, entropy, density, and age, are all exactly balanced for life. The velocity of light and the polarity of water are just right for life. These mathematical regularities are essential for life and, as far as we know, found nowhere else in the universe. The anthropic principle suggests a finely tuned universe designed for human life.

Oxford zoologist Richard Dawkins mocks the notion that this convergence of just-right factors points to God. He ridicules the notion of the "Divine Knob-Twiddler." As far as he is concerned, the anthropic principle is just the way the universe happens to be. "It provides a rational, design-free explanation for the fact that we find ourselves in a situation propitious to our existence."[2] How all of these balances, ratios, proportions and parameters came to be no one knows and is, according to Dawkins, best explained by luck. Dawkins reasons that if the odds were, let's say, a billion to one that life arose spontaneously, life is still probable because there's between 1 billion and 30 billion planets in our galaxy, and over a 100 billion galaxies in the universe. Thus, "a billion billion is a conservative estimate of the number of available planets in the universe."[3]

He continues,

> If the odds of life originating spontaneously on a planet were a
> billion to one against, nevertheless that stupefyingly improb-

able event would still happen on a billion planets. The chance of finding any one of those billion life-bearing planets recalls the proverbial needle in a haystack. But we don't have to go out of our way to find a needle because (back to the anthropic principle) any beings capable of looking must necessarily be sitting on one of those prodigiously rare needles before they even start the search.[4]

For Dawkins, sheer luck and chance account for the origin of life and natural selection explains the diversity of life. In his own words:

> The evolution of life is a completely different case from the origin of life because, to repeat, the origin of life was (or could have been) a unique event which had to happen only once. The adaptive fit of species to their separate environments, on the other hand, is millionfold, and ongoing. . . . We can deal with the unique origin of life by postulating a very large number of planetary opportunities. Once that initial stroke of luck has been granted—and the anthropic principle most decisively grants it to us—natural selection takes over: and natural selection is emphatically not a matter of luck.[5]

Contrary to Dawkin's notions of luck and probability, the anthropic principle bears silent testimony to the design and meaning of the universe. The atheist turns to notions of luck and fate; the theist turns to miracle and faith. For Job to write his meditation on science from the ash heap seems far more convincing than speculations about luck from the ivory tower. The fact that Job should write about science and wisdom is consistent with the miracle of life itself.

MEDITATION ON SCIENCE

By the time we reach this stage in the dialogue between Job and his would-be counselors, everyone has lost his temper.

The give-and-take has left Job's counselors-turned-torment-ers exhausted and, at long last, silent. But Job is still going strong. Nothing has changed in his circumstances. He remains homeless, friendless, naked, ulcerous, and in despair. Neverthe-less, he reflects a depth of insight and passion that his would-be counselors cannot even touch. Amazingly, Job has acquired new strength and insight. As the process has dragged on, Job has become more focused and confident, while his counselors have become mean and distraught. He has become stronger as they have become weaker.

You recall that Satan accused God of programming Job for obedience. Satan's view corresponds to those who view the human person as a mere product of his environment, best explained by some form of spiritual or scientific determin-ism. Whether the cause is fatalistic or naturalistic, spiritual or secular, makes little difference. Either way the human person is reduced and dehumanized. The modern equivalent to ancient superstitions is atheistic naturalism and bio-determinism.

When Satan finishes with Job, Job is stripped bare. He has no earthly reason, no human rationale for remaining true to God. Much of Job's dialogue is his passionate, heart-rending account of his total destitution. Every gift and blessing is gone. He feels he is in bondage in every way: physically, socially, spiritually, materially, and emotionally. He feels God-forsaken, abandoned by the God he seeks to love and obey. Nevertheless, he remains faithful! He cries out, "Though he slay me, yet will I hope in him; I will surely defend my ways to his face" (13:15).

He longs to make his case before God, confident that he will be vindicated (13:18). Even though God is silent, Job hopes in God. "But he knows the way that I take; when he has tested me, I will come forth as gold" (23:10). Unbeknown to Job, his faithful response meant so much to God that God allows evident injustice to take place to prove that Job is not programmed, but free. And in the midst of this horrible bondage and despair, Job continues to give powerful proof of his freedom. The Lord God boasts of his servant to Satan, "...He still maintains his integrity, though you incited me against him to ruin him without reason" (2:3). Job did not know why he was being afflicted and the absence of that knowledge made his freedom complete. He may not have known it at the time, but he was never more free than when he sat on the ash heap!

By chapter 28, his so-called friends have talked themselves into despair, while Job's courage and confidence have only grown and deepened. We sense his growing capacity to reflect on the wisdom and sovereignty of God. Against all the meaningless talk that he has been subjected to, Job proclaims, "I will teach you about the power of God, the ways of the Almighty I will not conceal." (27:11).

The story moves from intense anguish and suffering to the cool detachment of scientific inquiry. Some may find the transition jarring, but the juxtaposition of spiritual despair and scientific objectivity is true to life. Job is aware that life goes on in spite of great suffering. Exploration and engineering are pursued unabated even though the war within continues. "Man is a maggot," Bildad shouts in despair (25:6), but from the ash heap Job argues otherwise. He marvels at the ingenuity and courage of miners who tunnel deep into the earth to retrieve precious metals—silver, gold, iron ore and gemstones. Only human beings are capable of such engineering feats. Falcons with their excellent vision cannot see beneath the earth and lions with their courage cannot go below the surface. Mining remains one of the most dangerous occupations known to man.

Job may be hinting that "the getting of wisdom will be equally strenuous and hazardous."[6] He may also be implying that wisdom like gold and silver lies hidden. "There is no suggestion that the author is disapproving, as if he thought that the energies spent on the search for material wealth would be better used in the quest of wisdom. His point is much simpler. Man's remarkable success as a miner shows how clever and intelligent he is; but, for all that, he has failed completely to unearth wisdom."[7] Science's capacity to bring hidden things to light is amazing. We should let the microbiologist write a Job-like meditation and encourage the astrophysicist to give poetic expression to the hidden mysteries of the cosmos.

Since Job's day we haven't gone all that much deeper into the earth. Science writer Bill Byrson writes,

> This distance from the surface of the Earth to the center is 3,959 miles, which isn't so very far...Our own attempts to penetrate toward the middle have been modest indeed. One or two South African gold mines reach to a depth of two miles, but most mines on Earth go no more than about a quarter of a mile beneath the surface. If the planet were an apple, we wouldn't yet have broken through the skin. Indeed, we haven't even come close.[8]

Scientists believe that the earth is made up of two cores—a solid inner core and liquid outer core. Since no one has been able to explore below the earth's mantle, this knowledge is indirect. The pressures at the center of the Earth are three million times those found at the surface. The temperature is estimated at 7,000° F to 13,000° F—about as hot as the surface of the Sun.[9] The amazing thing about our scientific knowledge seems to be that the more we discover, the more we realize how much we don't know.

Job is impressed with the scientific and technological break-throughs of his day, but rather than squelching the questions related to meaning and purpose, science only heightens his quest for meaning.

> But where can wisdom be found? Where does understanding dwell? No mortal comprehends its worth; it cannot be found in the land of the living. The deep says, 'It's not in me'; the sea says, 'It's not with me' (28:12–14).

Good science is not afraid of the question of meaning and purpose. Former Dean of Yale Medical School, the late Lewis Thomas, was honest enough to say what many scientists hesitate to admit:

> I cannot make my peace with the randomness doctrine: I cannot abide the notion of purposelessness and blind chance in nature. And yet I do not know what to put in its place for the quieting of my mind. It is absurd to say that a place like this place is absurd, when it contains, in front of our eyes, so many billions of different forms of life, each one in its way absolutely perfect, all linked together to form what would surely seem to an outsider a huge spherical organism. We talk—some of us anyway—about the absurdity of the human situation, but we do this because we do not know how we fit in, or what we are for.[10]

When we look for something that is not there (because its not where we are looking for it) it is tempting to conclude that it doesn't exist. We would never think to look for our self-worth in our garage. Such an approach is neither scientific nor valid because we are looking for it in the wrong place. This is Job's point in one of the oldest books of the Bible, namely that the meaning of life is not found in the nature of things. Naturalism, scientism and historicism all try to do the same thing: by the use of human learning and genius to discover life's inner meaning in the nature of things and in historical processes. "In the conditions produced by a century or so of Naturalism, plain people are being forced to bear burdens which plain people were never expected to bear before. We must get the truth for ourselves or go without it."[11]

Wendell Berry exposes the "radical influence of reductive science" in *Life Is a Miracle: An Essay Against Modern Superstition*. Berry contends, "For quite a while it has been possible for a free and thoughtful person to see that to treat life as mechanical or predictable or understandable is to reduce it. Now, almost suddenly, it is becoming clear that to reduce life to the scope of our understanding (whatever 'model' we use) is inevitably to enslave it, make property of it, and put it up for sale. This is to give up on life, to carry it beyond change and redemption, and to increase the proximity of despair . . . To treat life as less than a miracle is to give up on it."[12]

Berry seeks to expose the ideological captivity of modern culture by a form of science (scientism or 'science-and-technology') that contends it has all the answers. Edward O. Wilson's *Consilience* or Richard Dawkins' *The God Delusion* epitomize this "religious faith in the power of science to know all things and solve all problems, whereupon the scientist may become an evangelist and go forth to save the world."[13] From such a point-of-view, life is inescapably deterministic and free will is an illusion. All talk of the soul or transcendence or the sacred is simply the "poetry of affirmation." He continues, "There are scientists, one must suppose, who know all about atoms or molecules or genes, or galaxies or planets or stars, but who do not know where they are geographically, historically, or ecologically. Our schools are turning out millions of graduates who do not know, in this sense, where they are."[14]

G. K. Chesterton judged materialism's explanation of life for its "insane simplicity."

> Now, speaking quite externally and empirically, we may say that the strongest and most unmistakable mark of madness is this combination between a logical completeness and a spiritual contraction. The lunatic's theory explains a large number of things, but it does not explain them in a large way. . . . I admit that your explanation explains a great deal; but what a great deal it leaves out! . . . As an explanation of the world, materialism has a sort of insane simplicity. It has the quality of the madman's argument; we have at once the sense of it covering everything and the sense of it leaving everything out.[15]

Job 28 celebrates human ingenuity and our ability to explore the hard-to-reach areas of nature. The deeper we explore nature, the more we discover her mind-boggling complexity. What was once thought to be a simple, nearly formless cell turns out to be a miniature cosmos! Biochemist Franklin Harold writes, "What the eye beholds depends on what it looks through." Today's instruments allow us to peer into the deep recesses of nature, and what we find is anything but simple. Harold describes a cell: "There are more than 2 million protein molecules per cell, potentially of four thousand kinds, and nearly a thousand species of small molecules; 300 million molecules in all, not counting water which makes up nine tenths of the cell's mass. All these jostle one another in a [cellular] volume of about one cubic micrometer."[16] Even the most high-tech, state-of-the-art automotive assembly plant is nothing compared to the so-called simple cell. When it comes to nature we never seem to arrive at the alleged simplicity that leads to complexity, nor do we ever discover that which is irreducibly complex. If nature appears absolutely resistant to reductionism, what should we expect of meaning itself?

What is true in the realm of science is even more true in the realm of meaning and purpose, wisdom and joy. C.S. Lewis wrote: "It is no good asking for a simple religion. After all, real things are not simple. They look simple, but they are not... If we ask for something more than simplicity, it is silly then to complain that the something more is not simple."[17] The human quest for meaning is not satisfied with technological breakthroughs, spectacular achievements, and breathtaking discoveries. Job 28 is a meditation on meaning, where it's not and where it can be found. It sums up "the failure of the human mind to arrive at the hidden wisdom" and "lays the foundation" for the revelation of God.[18]

Four thousand years ago, state-of-the-art science and engineering produced precious stones. Their value was derived more from their beauty than their utility, yet their wealth proved worthless in purchasing wisdom. Unearthed gold, onyx and topaz, acquired through intelligence and courage, equates today with micro-chips, internet search engines, the Airbus 380, cancer-killing smart bombs, and space-orbiting communications satellites. Then, and now, the products of science and technology cannot buy wisdom.

Job repeats his question:

> Where then does wisdom come from? Where does understanding dwell? It is hidden from the eyes of every living thing, concealed even from the birds in the sky. Destruction and Death say, 'Only a rumor of it has reached our ears' (28:20–22).

LORD OF THE UNIVERSE,
HOPE OF THE WORLD

Job leads us back to the *who* in order to answer the *what, when, how, and why*. "God understands the way to it and he alone knows where it dwells . . ." (Job 28:23). Meaning at its root is personal. Wisdom is ultimately relational—"embodied" by God. Wisdom personified, in Proverbs 8, is synonymous with the fear of the Lord and the presence of God. Wisdom-in-person is Joy, Love, and Life itself. The Knower precedes knowledge. We do not create meaning; meaning is revealed by God. Reason is a divinely fashioned instrument for recognizing truth, not inventing it. Human discovery can bring "hidden things to light," but the wisdom of God is "hidden from the eyes of every living thing" (28:11, 21). Wisdom is a gift from God, lest anyone should boast.

By faith—by sheer, naked, teeth-gritting, soul-clinging faith—Job remained faithful to God and expected justice from God. Even though Job is walking through the valley of the shadow of death, the glory of resurrection hope shines through. "I know that my Redeemer lives, and that in the end he will stand upon the earth. And after my skin has been destroyed, yet in my flesh I will see God; I myself will see him with my own eyes—I, and not another. How my heart yearns within me!" (19:25–27). Because his Redeemer lives, Job is confident not only in his own resurrection, but in the Sovereign control of God over all of creation.

Job anticipates God's response by attributing to God the wisdom necessary for weather systems and thunderstorms. In the end, the Lord breaks his silence and speaks to Job out of the storm, asking, "Who is this that obscures my plans with words without knowledge?" God does not sound very conciliatory or consoling. To some, God may even sound angry, but it is a mistake to confuse intensity with indignation and God's seriousness with God's wrath. God comes to Job as the Lord of the Universe, not as a counselor or as a therapist. God Almighty, holy and majestic, commissioned Job as a major warrior in the battle of righteousness. Job is approached by his Commander, not a chaplain. God makes no effort to explain. Congratulations for a job well done will come later.

The Lord does not condemn Job, nor does he call for Job's repentance. The opening question challenges Job's understanding, not his integrity: "Who is this that darkens my counsel with words without knowledge?" Job is ignorant and God sets the agenda. "He answers Job's questions with a deluge of counter-questions...Job is led out into the world...He invites Job to meet him almost as an equal, standing up *like a man*."[19] Job is enrolled in God's school of vocational holiness and the Professor knows his subject.

Even though everything in Job's life has appeared out of control, God is in control. The God of Job speaks: "Where were you when I laid the earth's foundation?. . . Have you ever given orders to the morning?. . . Have you comprehended the vast expanses of the earth?. . . Can you light up the light or put out the dark?" (38:4, 12, 18, 19).

Job is led out of his confined world of suffering into the large world of God's making. There he is challenged to explain the origin of the earth, the expanse of the sea, the light of dawn, the ocean depths, the formation of snow, lightning, and rain, and the order of the stars and seasons. God's questions sound more like exclamations, designed to inspire rather than interrogate. "Have you comprehended the vast expanses of the earth? Tell me, if you know all this" (38:18). Of course, Job had never even hinted that he knew the answers to these questions, let alone ever made such a claim, so when God says, "Surely you know, for you were already born! You have lived so many years!" (38:21), his intent is not to put Job down sarcastically, but to make a point emphatically. In other words, "Job! Let God be God!"

God's review of creation moves from the natural world to the animal world. Job is asked if he could satisfy the hunger of lions or provide food for the ravens. Is he able to explain the wild donkey, tame the wild ox, understand the ways of the ostrich, or take credit for the horse? Did he teach the hawk to fly or the eagle to soar? No, of course not, but God did, and the message comes through loud and clear, "Job! Let God be God!"

In the second round of God's revelation to Job, Yahweh briefly but strategically addresses his control over the moral realm. God raises the issue of justice at the center of his response to Job. Right in the middle of God's extended discourse on his creation and management of the universe, God asks, "Would you discredit my justice? Would you condemn me to justify yourself? Do you have an arm like God's, and can you voice thunder like his?" (40:8–9). Job is compelled to see that God's control extends not only to nature, but to human justice as well.

Job has said nothing that would contradict God's authority. He has never implied that he could set things right if he were in charge, but he has lamented God's apparent indifference to his plight. Now the thrust of God's message, and its "aggressive tone," brings Job "to the end of his quest by convincing him that he may and must hand the whole matter over completely to God more trustingly, less fretfully."[20] Job has to admit that whatever he had implied about God's indifference or thought about God's lack of concern was clearly wrong. The message is absolutely convincing. "Job! Let God be God!"

The climax of God's revelation comes with a graphic description of the behemoth (the untamable land creature), and leviathan (the terrifying sea creature). God doesn't have to look far to come up with creatures that test the limits of human control. Just try putting a nose ring in a hippopotamus or reeling in a crocodile. Who would be crazy enough to try tackling a charging hippo? (41:5). These creatures are described with imagination and humor in order to make the serious point that God is in control. "Who has a claim against me that I must pay? Everything under heaven belongs to me" (41:11). The message is unmistakable. "Job! Let God be God!"

Job's agonizing questions boil down to a passion for God. God's barrage of creation questions add up to a pronouncement of his sovereign control. It is not just anybody asking these creation questions; it is the Author of Life. God's response does not focus on the why and wherefore of suffering, but on the heart of the matter: Job's relationship with God. God's response does not treat Job like a hero, but a servant. Job is not exalted, he is educated, matured, brought closer to God. He is humbled before God, but not humiliated. Instead of letting go of God, he lets God be God.

Before others, God commends Job, both at the beginning and at the end. Job's ash heap faithfulness is vindicated by Almighty God, but when God and Job finally meet and go one on one, there is no doubt who is the Master and who is the servant. This is what Job wanted all along. He wanted to be back in fellowship with God. "Oh, for the days when I was in my prime, when God's intimate friendship blessed my house, when the Almighty was still with me . . . " (29:4). When God speaks,

SECOND THOUGHTS FOR SKEPTICS

"Brace yourself like a man; I will question you, and you shall answer me," Job does not cower, he bows. This is communion, not condemnation. He receives God's word as an invitation, not a threat. Job does not hesitate to humble himself before God Almighty. To do otherwise would have been a sin. His actions are completely in character. Job is speechless, "I am unworthy—how can I reply to you? I put my hand over my mouth" (40:4).

BRINGING HIDDEN THINGS TO LIGHT

Given what we know of the hidden things of nature, the truth of the Incarnation, while unexpected, fits in with the God of all Creation. If the value and significance of material existence and physical life needed any confirmation it got it in the Incarnation. Genesis 1:1 and John 1:1 are united in an absolutely essential revelation of truth and wisdom. "In the beginning God created the heavens and the earth" is linked to "In the beginning was the Word, and the Word was with God, and the Word was God. He was with God in the beginning. Through him all things were made; without him nothing was made that has been made" (John 1:1–3). The intersection of the physical universe and the moral universe by the Word made flesh is consistent and coherent with the Wisdom of God, which is simultaneously responsible for creation and outside of creation.

God deliberately made himself known in a way that nobody would have expected or even desired. Who would have anticipated the climactic revelation of God through the hidden way of the manger, the cross, and the empty tomb? Who would have expected that the invisible God would have come to us incognito, as a man upon whom the whole destiny of the human race depends? Søren Kierkegaard called this "the profoundest incognito, or the most impenetrable unrecognizableness that is possible; for the contradiction between being God and being an individual man is the greatest possible, the infinitely qualitative contradiction. But this is His will, His free determination, therefore an almightily maintained incognito."[21]

Many would prefer an idea of their own invention—an alternative explanation, independent of God's ways. On the surface we long for something simple—a good one-liner that makes sense to us. We'd like to take a page out of *Life's Little Instruction Book* and turn a blind eye to the complexity of the world. It is easier to be told, "It's not your fault," or "You are the secret to your joy and happiness" or "Believe in yourself" or "You can do anything you put your mind to." But life isn't like that.

C. S. Lewis observed, "If Christianity was something we were making up, of course we could make it easier. But it is not. We cannot compete, in simplicity, with people who are inventing religions. How could we? We are dealing with Fact. Of course anyone can be simple if he has no facts to bother about."[22] Albert Einstein is quoted as saying, "Everything should be made as simple as possible, but not simpler."

Why is there so much hidden in nature and why has it taken us so long to discover it? Why is there still so much hidden in nature, so that it seems like we have only just begun to explore the universe?

We might prefer our science more obvious and simple, just as we might prefer our theology more obvious and simple. Why the sublety of a covenant with Abraham, an exodus from oppression, a journey into the wilderness, a promised land, an exile to Babylon, a virginal conception, a voice crying in the wilderness, and a birth like none other? An "immense Zeus-like figure towering over us like a hundred Everests" (Norwood

Russell) would be fearfully convincing, but not the essence of redemptive love revealed in the Incarnation of God. God chose instead a single individual who became obedient to death— even death on a cross. The Lord of the Universe took our place in the grand scheme of things, became one of us, and sat with us on the human ash heap. The same God, who designed the cosmos and the cell, conceived the way of salvation and went by way of the cross. God emptied the tomb and filled life with meaning. God chose not to blow us away or bully us into sub- mission, but to invite us to himself through the personal story of his own submission, sacrifice, and redemption. He comes to us in disguise, not to deceive us nor overwhelm us with his power, but to convince us of his love. John 3:16 is hardly simple but it is profoundly true.

6

ALL THINGS HOLD TOGETHER

"The Son is the image of the invisible God, the firstborn
over all creation. For in him all things were created:
things in heaven and on earth, visible and invisible,
whether thrones or powers or rulers or authorities; all
things have been created through and for him. He is
before all things, and in him all things hold together."

Colossians 1:15–17

Job's ash heap theology leads himself and us ultimately to a theology of glory. His journey was long and painful, but Job ended up in a state of praise. Contemplating the wonders of God's physical and moral universe in the context of pain and suffering fills Job, and ought to fill us, with a powerful new sense of confidence, wisdom, wonder and humility. By placing his suffering in relationship to the Sovereign Lord, Job opens his eyes to the glory of God. The agony and the absurdity of the ash heap give way to adoration and worship:

> "I know that you can do all things: no purpose of yours can
> be thwarted. You asked, 'Who is this that obscures my plans
> without knowledge?' Surely I spoke of things I did not under-
> stand, things too wonderful for me to know. You said, 'Listen

SECOND THOUGHTS FOR SKEPTICS

now, and I will speak; I will question you, and you shall answer
me.' My ears had heard of you but now my eyes have seen you.
Therefore I despise myself and repent in dust and ashes" (Job
42:2–6).

Job's life is a tutorial in the truth of God's saving and sustaining presence. From his "hospital room" he verifies the truth
that God "sustains all things by his powerful word" (Hebrews
1:3) and that "through Him all things were made; without
Him nothing was made that has been made" (John 1:3). In the
end, there is a wonderful convergence in Job's experience that
points forward to the cross and the resurrection. Job's experience works like a parable, thrown alongside a larger reality.
He helps us "get it." Through the Incarnation, God descends
into our suffering humanity, joins us on the ash heap, takes up
this mean battle with Satan, and goes to the cross. The Lord
of Glory is crucified, but the cross is not the last word and the
resurrection is not a wild card played at the end. There is an un-
inventable coherence between the life, death and resurrection
of Jesus and the truth of the universe. The power of the resurrection fits with the wonder and meaning of life as we know it,
from the science of creation to the justice of the moral order.

We long to reunite in our thoughts and actions what God
has joined together: creation and redemption, discipline and
devotion, theology and holiness, intellectual competence and
burning love, work and wonder, humility and beauty. A
"sitting" theology cannot do justice to this convergence. Only a
"kneeling" theology will do.[1] All things hold together. If the old
creation inspired a theology of glory, just think of the worship
inspired by the new creation.

THINKING IS REQUIRED

Our thesis is that there is a real correspondence between the Resurrection of Christ and a meaningful life. This truth cannot be contemplated and appreciated apart from thinking deeply. Yet this kind of thinking, even among Christians is rare today. Too many of our brightest Christian students go off to university without any real awareness of a coherent biblical view of life. Instead of a well-informed Christian worldview shaping their lives, they become subject to the ideological captivity of the university.

Conceptual thinking is an acquired skill. Children do not automatically process abstract thought. They are more attuned to the moment than to meaning. They are more preoccupied with feeling good than with understanding goodness. They understand what hurts long before they contemplate suffering. Their ability to think conceptually, to rise above the immediate, tangible, temporal fact and embrace a larger truth is a measure of their maturity.

Thought has fallen on hard times because it is allegedly boring, but it need not be that way. Jesus rightly criticized the abstract thinking of the Pharisees. They epitomized a literalistic, wooden, and burdensome form of negative abstract teaching. One reason the crowds were drawn to Jesus was because he taught with authority. He cut through the pedantic proof texting and scribal legalese and declared the truth. Jesus was not afraid to carry the message by way of metaphor and analogy into deep conceptual thought. He creatively linked the tangible to the intangible, the visible to the invisible, and the concrete to the conceptual.

Jesus insisted on an integrative understanding of truth that united material and spiritual realties in himself. When he performed the miracle of feeding the five thousand, he deliberately drove the message beyond the tolerance of his audience. Nobody found the message easy. Instead of working his audience, making sure everybody kept up and nobody was turned off, Jesus deliberately shocked and challenged. Without clarifying definitions and careful explanations, not to mention intensity-relieving humor, Jesus focused the Bread of Life and Passover Lamb metaphors upon himself. When Jesus said, "Unless you eat my body and drink my blood you have no life in you," he plunged his audience into truth too deep for humanistic consumption.

THE GOD OF ALL TRUTH

The descriptive passage below claims that Jesus Christ is central to our understanding of science, history and personal fulfillment. This goes well beyond devotional speech that sounds good when read in a worship service. This powerful confession is a bold epistemological declaration that was meant to revolutionize the way we think and live. We cannot dismiss this as religious rhetoric and then go on with our thinking as if this has no bearing on how we do science and carry out our personal ambitions.

> The Son is the image of the invisible God, the firstborn over *all* creation. For in him *all* things were created: things in heaven and on earth, visible and invisible, whether thrones or powers or rulers or authorities; *all* things have been created through and for him. He is before *all* things, and in him *all* things hold together. And he is the head of the body, the church; he is the beginning and the firstborn from among the dead, so that in *everything* he might have the supremacy. For God was pleased to have *all* his fullness dwell in him, and through him to reconcile to himself

all things, whether things on earth or things in heaven, by making peace through his blood, shed on the cross.

As the rest of Paul's letter to the church at Colosse unfolds, it becomes apparent why the apostle prefaced his practical counsel with this eloquent and powerful description of Christ. He presents the supremacy of Christ over all creation and redemption. Jesus Christ is the source and goal of all creation and the source and goal of all redemption. The early church was already battling early forms of Gnosticism. This dualistic worldview contended that the transcendent and holy God had nothing to do with the material world. The material world was inferior, inconsequential, and separated from the highly valued spiritual realm. Some Gnostics argued that physical life was so inconsequential that the body could be indulged without consequence to one's spiritual life. Other gnostics argued that evil was so tied to material existence that ordinary life needed to be strictly regulated and harshly treated. In either case, the spiritual life was divorced from the material world.

Since we face similar dualistic worldviews and lifestyles today, we want to pay attention to this early Christian confession, because it proclaims that the gift of Christ is the gift of total truth. In Christ, there is no division or separation between science and religion, between secular history and sacred history, between nature and grace. There is no dichotomy between personal values and public facts, between personal convictions and scientific knowledge, between subjective feelings and objective facts. As there was and is no division in Christ, there is no division in truth. The early church gave considerable thought as to how best to express the meaning of the Incarnation. The Chalcedonian Creed (451) confessed that our Lord Jesus Christ is "truly God and truly man . . . like us in all things except without sin; begotten from the Virgin Mary, the Mother of God, as regards his manhood; one and the same Christ, Son, Lord, only-begotten, made known in two natures without confusion, without change, without division, without separation." This description of the being of Christ, "made known in two natures without confusion, without change, without division, without separation," is also a fitting description of the truth of Christ. The gospel of Christ supports this inclusive, all-encompassing understanding of truth as well. Jesus affirmed the reality of total truth when he said, "I am the way and the truth and the life. No one comes to the Father except through me" (John 14:6). If all truth is God's truth and Jesus is Lord of all, then Christianity cannot be restricted to a private sphere of personal subjective devotion and religious belief.

Paul's confession of Christ unites creation and redemption under the supremacy of Christ. This early confession of Christ will not allow us to do what one Bible teacher in a Christian high school did in a class of two hundred students. He drew a heart on one side of the blackboard and a brain on the other. He explained that the heart and the brain represented two separate categories of meaning. The heart is what we use for religion and the brain is what we use for science.[2] There are not two types or two realms of truth. We cannot divorce our significance, meaning, purpose and value from the material world of empirical fact and cognitive reason. Wonder and awe coexist in the same realm as history and science. Faith and reason belong together in one unified understanding of truth.

The evidence of creation makes it difficult to separate the Creator from his creation. This is why those who deny the connection have to insist on nature alone or in a two-story theory of truth. A split-level view of truth contends that objective, scientific, and empirical truth is altogether different from subjective, personal, and value oriented truth. The Bible, however, claims all truth as God's truth and affirms the unity of truth. Nature cannot be divorced from her Creator and history cannot be separated from the Lord of the Nations. Moreover, we cannot know the Creator apart from the Redeemer.

Writer Tim Stafford describes an object lesson that Pastor Stephen Belynskyj uses with new members of his church. He starts with a jar full of beans and he asks them to guess how many beans are in the jar. On a big pad of paper he writes down their estimates. Then, next to those estimates, he helps them make another list: their favorite songs. When the lists are complete, he reveals the actual number of beans in the jar. The whole class looks over the guesses to see which estimate was closest to being right. Belynskyj then turns to the list of favorite songs. "And which one of these is closest to being right?" he asks. The students protest that there is no "right answer"; a person's favorite song is purely a matter of taste. Belynskyj, who holds a Ph.D. in philosophy from Notre Dame, says, "When you decide what to believe in terms of your faith, is that more like guessing the number of beans, or more like choosing your favorite song?"

Always, Belynskyj says, from old as well as young, he gets the same answer: choosing one's faith is more like choosing a favorite song. He then proceeds to argue them out of it, because faith in Christ is not a question of taste, but a matter of fact. "Favorite-song theology" leaves the impression that everyone has a right to their opinions when it comes to faith in Christ. There is no right or wrong, true or false, because it is a matter of taste.[3]

Is faith in Christ mainly a matter of subjective experience, controlled by what I think and feel and choose to believe, or is it a matter of objective reality? Many people operate on the basis of two distinct ways of knowing. There is a public world of facts and a private world of opinions. In the world of science, math, and the IRS, everyone ought to be held to an objective standard, but when it comes to values and faith there is no universal authority, no real right or wrong. The apostle Paul warns us not to betray the nature of truth: "See to it that no one takes you captive through hollow and deceptive philosophy, which depends on human tradition and the basic principles of this world rather than on Christ" (Colossians 2:8). The Christian faith is not a folk religion. Conversion is not a heightened state of consciousness, but a life commitment to the objective truth of Christ. Moral absolutes are true whether we like them or not. True proclamation requires discernment and understanding to defend against the blending and mixing of hollow and deceptive philosophy with the gospel. Paul's mission statement holds us accountable for the sake of Christ and Christian maturity. British author Harry Blamires writes,

> The Christian mind has an overriding sense that the truth it clings to is supernaturally grounded, revealed not manufactured, imposed not chosen, authoritative, objective and irresistible. If the Christian comes before the secular mind claiming less for Christian truth than is its due, he not only betrays the Faith, he contributes to the erosion of the Christian mind. The Christian Faith has to be defended for the right reason. Too long we have been defending it for the wrong reason, trying to win a place for it in the secular esteem by claiming that it ministers to ends served by the secular welfare, and that it can be turned into a personal philosophy adequate to give solace to a secular mentality through a secularist career.

We have to insist that the Christian Faith is something solider, harder, and tougher than even Christians like to think. Christianity is not a nice comforting story that we make up as we go along accommodating the demands of harsh reality with the solace of a cherished reverie. It is not a cosy day-dream manufactured by each person more or less to suit his own taste. It is a matter of hard fact. We Christians appreciate its hardness just as much as those outside the Church. We are as fully aware of its difficulties as the outsiders are. We know that, in a sense, Christianity leaves us with an awful lot to swallow. No Christian, thinking Christianly, divesting himself of the easy self-deceptions of secularist thinking, will pretend that Christianity is an easy faith—easy to accept, easy to explore, easy to rest in, easy to explain. It isn't. We must outdo the unbelievers in agreeing with them on that subject. We must stand at their side and look with them at this thing, the Christian Faith, and vie with them in detaching ourselves from it. "You find it difficult? So do I. 'You find it awkward? So do I. You find it unattractive? That's exactly how I often find it myself, especially round about 7 o'clock on a Sunday morning. You think it a thundering nuisance? In a way I quite agree with you. It is a nuisance at times, especially in Lent. But it's *true*, you know."[4]

The Author/Artist/Composer of all creation and the Savior/Redeemer/Lord of all salvation are one and the same. The history of nature and the history of redemption are revelations of the same God. Each reinforces the wonder, awe, beauty and truth of the other. Chosen in Christ "before the creation of the world to be holy and blameless in his sight" unites the physical and material creation with the spiritual and historical reality—all of which is designed by God (Ephesians 1:4). This is not a rhetorical flourish, but statement of fact. The God and Father of our Lord Jesus Christ, who authored DNA and ordained redemption, has purposed "to bring unity to all things in heaven and on earth under Christ" (Ephesians 1:10). Everything in nature and redemption is moving forward according to plan—"the plan of him who works out everything in conformity with the purpose of his will." Albert Einstein asserted that "without belief in the inner harmony of the world there could be no science."[5] The apostle Paul goes further and asserts that the God and Father of our Lord Jesus Christ has not only created an inner harmony but an ultimate convergence. The cosmos is not a coincidence. History is moving toward its fulfillment.

We have a huge decision to make: are we the holy possession of God in Christ, personally chosen by God, predestined for communion with God, adopted into the community of God's people, recipients of God's grace, redeemed by his personal sacrifice on our behalf, and signed, sealed and delivered by the promised Holy Spirit, OR are we the accidental product of an impersonal universe, subject to blind chance and random forces, existing in a sphere of energy devoid of promise, plan, purpose and fulfillment?

Most Americans say they believe in God but do they believe in the God and Father of our Lord Jesus? It appears that many people are trying to live in a no-man's land, half-way between a real relationship with God in Christ and surviving as a cosmic accident. They can't bring themselves to say there is no God but they can't bring themselves to accept the God who seeks to bless them—the living Lord God who is responsible for creation and redemption.

God is not a theory to be postulated for the sake of getting on with life. The generic god of popular imagination is like the proverbial straw man, a victim easily dismissed. For some time, secularists have rejected their own idea of god without grappling with the God of the Bible. When Napoleon asked French mathematician and physicist Laplace about God, Laplace quipped,

"I have no need of that hypothesis." Many echo Woody Allen's line, from his film *Crimes and Misdemeanors*, "God is a luxury I cannot afford." As long as the term *god* is an idea or an image "made by human design" (Acts 17:29) it deserves to be rejected. There is no generic god that can be known before God the Father, Son and Holy Spirit.

Some have claimed that Einstein believed in God, but it appears he made an important distinction between a generalized notion of god and the personal God revealed in the Bible. He may have given us some quotable lines, such as, "Science without religion is lame, religion without science is blind," but he was not a believer in the God of the Bible. For the record he wrote, "I do not believe in a personal God and I have never denied this but have expressed it clearly. If something is in me which can be called religious then it is the unbounded admiration for the structure of the world, so far as our science can reveal it."[6]

Karl Barth was one of the leading theologians of the twentieth century. Commenting on the Apostle's Creed, he claimed that we can only know the God of Creation by knowing the God of Redemption.

> I believe in God, the Father Almighty, Creator of heaven and earth. When we approach the truth which the Christian Church confesses in the word 'Creator', then everything depends on our realizing that we find ourselves here, as well, confronted by the mystery of faith, in respect of which knowledge is real solely through God's revelation. The first article of faith in God the Father and His work is not a sort of 'forecourt' of the Gentiles, a realm in which Christians and Jews and Gentiles, believers and unbelievers are beside one another and to some extent stand together in the presence of a reality concerning which there might be some measure of agreement, in describing it as the work of God the Creator. What the meaning of God the

Creator is and what is involved in the work of creation, is in itself not less hidden from us men than everything else that is contained in the Confession. We are not nearer to believing in God the Creator, than we are to believing that Jesus Christ was conceived by the Holy Spirit and born of the Virgin Mary. It is not the case that the truth about God the Creator is directly accessible to us and that only the truth of the second article needs revelation. But in the same sense in both cases we are faced with the mystery of God and His work, and the approach to it can only be one and the same.

It is impossible to separate the knowledge of God the Creator and of His work from the knowledge of God's dealings with man. Only when we keep before us what the triune God has done for us in Jesus Christ can we realize what is involved in God the Creator and His work. Creation is the temporal analogue, taking place outside God, of that event in God himself by which God is the Father of the Son . . . what God does as the Creator can in the Christian sense only be seen and understood as a reflection, as a shadowing forth of this inner divine relationship between God the Father and the Son . . . . Knowledge of creation is knowledge of God and consequently knowledge of faith in the deepest and ultimate sense. It is not just a vestibule in which natural theology might find a place.[7]

CREATION & REDEMPTION

Not only is God's workmanship evident in redemption as it is in creation, but it is evident in similar ways. Upon closer examination both creation and redemption evolved slowly over time, each with greater complexity than we might have imagined. Both involved an underlying theme of suffering and sacrifice. The parallels between creation and redemption are fascinating and point to a common author and architect. Relative to the average human life span of approximately 650,000 hours, creation and redemption operate in slow time—very slow time for creation, and even salvation history, at least from our perspective, seems to have been drawn out. Earth's presence is minuscule in cosmic space and from 30,000 feet, overpopulation does not seem to be the problem that it appears to be from an ecological perspective.

In a work of art there can be plenty of blank space. In music there are rests. In poetry much is left unsaid in order to say exactly what should be said. In the cosmos, deep space defies the imagination. "The average distance between stars out there is 20 million million miles."[8] Physicists explain that what appears to the naked eye to be solid matter is mostly space. This is true in the history of salvation as well. Silence frames great eons of unmarked time. Centuries pass without a word, but the story continues.

The title of J. B. Phillips's spiritual classic *Your God is Too Small*, could be changed to *Your God is Too Fast*. We would like God to do things quickly, but from looking at creation and redemption it appears that God likes to do things slowly, at least from our perspective. Some feel that the only way to honor God is by concluding that he created the cosmos in six days, but that doesn't appear to be the case. The apostle Peter warns us not to forget this one thing: "With the Lord a day is like a thousand years, and a thousand years are like a day. The Lord is not slow in keeping his promise, as some understand slowness. Instead he is patient with you, not wanting anyone to perish, but everyone to come to repentance" (2 Peter 3:8–9).

Added to these signature perspectives of space, silence and slowness, is an amazing process of selectivity. Both creation and redemption narrow down to an unexpected specificity. C. S. Lewis describes this selectivity in creation:

> Out of enormous space a very small portion is occupied by matter at all. Of all the stars, perhaps very few, perhaps only

one, have planets. Of the planets in our own system probably only one supports organic life. In the transmission of organic life, countless seeds and spermatozoa are emitted: some few are selected for the distinction of fertility. Among species only one is rational. Within that species only a few attain excellence of beauty, strength, or intelligence.[9]

What is true of creation is also true of redemption. The covenant of love is not extended to the best and the brightest but to the smallest and the weakest (Deuteronomy 7:7–9). But it is not a matter of God playing favorites. The selectivity is for the sake of salvation. "The 'chosen' people are chosen not for their own sake (certainly not for their own honor or pleasure) but for the sake of the *unchosen*. Abraham is told that 'in his seed' (the chosen nation) 'all nations will be blest.' That nation has been chosen to bear a heavy burden. Their sufferings are great but, as Isaiah recognized, their sufferings heal others."[10]

The continuation of creation and the progress of salvation history run along a knife edge. Both simultaneously hang in the balance. We live in an incredibly fine tuned universe. The slightest change in gravity or electromagnetic forces or nuclear forces would render our universe inhospitable to life. What is true of creation is also true of redemption. The history of salvation has come perilously close to a premature end on numerous occasions, and would have, if it had not been for the sovereign plan of God.

Along with *slowness, space/silence*, and *selectivity*, comes a fourth factor: *suffering*. The underlying theme of Creation as we know it and Redemption as it has been revealed to us is suffering and death. The principle of biology is death and decay and the first principle of reconciliation is the cross. Life is fallen and fragile, and all creation groans. "For the creation was subjected to frustration, not by its own choice, but by the

ALL THINGS HOLD TOGETHER

will of the one who subjected it, in hope that the creation itself will be liberated from its bondage to decay and brought into the freedom and glory of the children of God" (Romans 8:20–21).

There is plenty of advanced warning throughout the history of salvation that God is going to intervene personally in the human dilemma. Job's experience implies it. Abraham's near sacrifice of Isaac suggests it. Isaiah's prophecy of the Suffering Servant spells it out and David's lament cries out for it. Vicariousness is built into the whole sacrificial system. By the time Jesus came we should have expected it. "The Sinless Man suffers for the sinful, and, in their degree, all good men for all bad men."[11] It is these characteristics of creation and redemption, the composite nature of the person, the pattern of descent, the selectiveness of God in choosing a planet and choosing a people, and the vicariousness in God's sacrificial system that all point to the reasonableness of the Incarnation of God. Christ is the 'beginning' and the 'firstborn' in resurrection as well as in creation. Therefore he is preeminent in all things. He is the source and goal of all of creation and all of redemption.

A SACRAMENTAL VIEW OF LIFE

There is more to life than meets the eye. When C. S. Lewis wrote *The Chronicles of Narnia* toward the end of his career, it was as a fitting climax to a large and diverse body of work. Lewis' scholars see a great unity in all he wrote. He wrote as a classical medievalist, a literary critic, an apologist, a theologian, and an imaginative story teller, but all his work conveys a certain presence of mind, a mind filled with wonder, a mind truly open to the truth of God. He was convinced that one of the best ways to present the truth about life was through the imagination. Lewis reasoned that when he became a man he put away childish things, one of which was the fear of being childlike. He cultivated the capacity of wonder. He took his Lord seriously, "Truly I tell you, unless you change and become like little children, you will never enter the kingdom of heaven" (Matthew 18:3).

All of life is of God and belongs to God. Creation and Redemption converge to infuse life with sacred significance. "He is before all things, and in him all things hold together" and all things are reconciled through him, "by making peace through his blood shed on the cross." The Divine purpose— bringing unity to all things in heaven and on earth in Christ, overcomes the great divorce between our fallen-ness and our fulfillment. In Christ the physical and the spiritual, the temporal and the eternal, the mundane and the devotional are united. Redemptive love rescues romantic love, integrates truth and beauty, unifies families and races, and infuses meaning in ordinary daily life. This unity depends on the absolute singularity of Christ.

There is a difference between this unique singularity and specialization. The specialist takes pride in studying one aspect of life exhaustively. The sacramentalist takes comfort in knowing the center of life personally. In Christ we have the lens through which we can examine life from every angle, without fear of meaninglessness—without the dread of nothingness.

Dante celebrates this sacramental vision toward the end of *Paradise* in *The Divine Comedy*:

> O Light Supreme, so far beyond the reach
> of mortal understanding, to my mind
> relend now some small part of Your own Self,
> and give to my tongue eloquence enough
> to capture just one spark of all Your glory

that I may leave for future generations;
for, by returning briefly to my mind
and sounding, even faintly, in my verse,
more of Your might will be revealed to men.
If I had turned my eyes away, I think,
from the sharp brilliance of the living Ray
which they endured, I would have lost my senses.
And this, as I recall, gave me more strength
to keep on gazing till I could unite
my vision with the Infinite Worth I saw.
O grace abounding and allowing me to dare
to fix my gaze on the Eternal Light,
so deep my vision was consumed in It!
I saw how it contains within its depths
all things bound in a single book of love
of which creation is the scattered leaves:
how substance, accident, and their relation
were fused in such a way that what I now
describe is but a glimmer of that Light.
I know I saw the universal form,
the fusion of all things, for I can feel,
while speaking now, my heart leap up in joy.[12]

Canto XXXIII, lines 67–93

Harry Blamires says it well,

The Christian Faith presents a sacramental view of life. It
shows life's positive richness as derivative from the supernatural. It teaches us that to create beauty or to experience beauty,
to recognize truth or to discover truth, to receive love or to
give love, is to come into contact with realities that express
the Divine Nature. At a time when Christianity is so widely
misrepresented as life-rejecting rather than life-affirming, it is
urgently necessary to right the balance."[13]

We should want to take the apostle Paul more seriously
when he says that "if anyone is in Christ, the new creation has

come: The old has gone, the new is here!" (2 Corinthians 5:17). Lewis' description underscores the convergence of creation and redemption. Redemption means the evolution of a whole new person: "People often ask when the next step in evolution— the step to something beyond man—will happen. But on the Christian view, it has happened already."[14] In Christ, the new kind of person has already arrived.

There is a little word in our text that makes all the difference. It is the word "all" and it is repeated seven times. The simple word *all* with its all-encompassing reality is the key. Unless we embrace the truth of this tiny word completely, we will never know the health and wholeness of an undivided heart and mind. Jesus is Lord of all; all creation is his by right of inheritance, design, creation and redemption. The tremendous truth of this confession is that in Christ we participate in this all. This is the *all* that must not be evaded but embraced by all who desire to please God, because God's holy claim rests equally on all. So that "whatever you do, whether in word or deed, do it all in the name of the Lord Jesus, giving thanks to God the Father through him" (Colossians 3:17). This is the *all* that believes that Jesus accomplished *all* on the Cross. Judging from a worldly perspective, Jesus' life ended in tragic failure on the cross. In the moment, all was lost, hopelessly lost. Yet eternally understood, Jesus "had in the same moment accomplished all, and on that account said, with eternity's wisdom, 'It is finished.'"[15]

This is the *all* that is willing to *suffer all* for God. This is the *all* of a covenant love that is grandly inclusive of all we are and will be. This is the all-encompassing commitment to love and serve Christ, worship and cherish him in prosperity and in adversity; in sorrow and in happiness; in sickness and in health;

and forsaking all others, be united with him for all eternity. This is the *all* that knows no limits.

> He who did not spare his own Son,
> but gave him up for us all—
> how will he not also, along with him,
> graciously give us all things? (Romans 8:32)

THE EMPTY TOMB
AND THE NEW BIOLOGY

*"Unless I see the nail marks in his hands and
put my finger where the nails were, and put
my hand into his side, I will not believe."*

John 20:25

S alvation history moves toward the cross out of a necessity
designed by the Lord of history. From Genesis to Revelation,
the meaning of the cross and the mystery of the atonement
unfold under the sovereign direction of God. We are prepared
for the cross through images, events, allusions, symbols,
parables, prophecies, and poetry. Every form, phase, type, and
strata of the Bible points to the cross. From the Garden of Eden
to the return of the exiles, from Babylon and the birth of Christ
to the Garden of Gethsemane, we are moving toward the cross.

To most historians the meaning of the cross is by no means
obvious. The divine necessity is hidden in the course of human
affairs. Current events have always been far more significant to
history's newsmakers than what God was doing and revealing.
Yet to those who have eyes to see and ears to hear, *history* testifies

to the inevitability of the cross and God's revelation declares its meaning. *Salvation is woven into the very fabric of history.*

As *history* moved toward the cross, *creation* moves toward the Resurrection. Salvation is woven into the very fabric of nature, as well. Of course the cross and the resurrection cannot be separated from one another—both are revealed by God, both are space/time historical events, and both are embraced by faith. Moreover, both defy division into physical and spiritual categories.

Our conviction is this: if the history of God's revelation points to the cross, the nature of God's creation points to the resurrection. We are prepared for the resurrection through the "big bang," the language of DNA, the human quest for knowledge, the Periodic Table, mathematical patterns and formulas, the human capacity for beauty, the anthropic principle of the universe, the incredible complexity of the living cell, and the meaning of the human drama.

The divine necessity of the resurrection is hidden in the mystery and complexity of nature. Philosophical commitments to reductionism and materialism preclude the possibility of even entertaining the notion that the beauty, complexity, and meaning of creation can be derived from anything other than "a more-or-less farcical outcome of a chain of accidents" reaching back in time.[1] Yet to those who have eyes to see and ears to hear *creation* testifies to the logical coherence and meaningful power of the resurrection. *God's revelation declares its meaning in the context of nature's wonder and human need. Salvation is woven into the very fabric of creation.*

The empty tomb of Jesus is emblematic of *all* meaningfulness. It is the only emptiness that fills history and creation with meaning. The bodily resurrection of Jesus rolls away the stone of nihilism, materialism, and reductionism and opens the way to the beauty, complexity, and mystery of life itself. Christ's death atones for our sins; Christ's life assures our salvation. Jesus Christ is the source and goal of all creation, and the source and goal of all redemption.

Our natural tendency may be to reduce the Gospel down to human interest stories that say more about us than they do about the Lord. Why settle for inspirational talks that feature a cameo appearance of Jesus when we could explore the whole counsel of God? We would never think of equating a television sitcom with the drama of real life. Why do we settle for anything less than in-depth thinking and preaching when it comes to the reality of the resurrection of Christ? We should want to explore the complexity of God's creation and revel in the mystery of God's resurrection power. Instead of dumbing down the Gospel we should be striving to understand its marvelous depth.

Paradoxically, as we become more sophisticated in our methods of communication we seem to become more simplistic in our communication of the Gospel. As the speed and accessibility of communications has increased, so has our apparent impatience with the meaning of the Gospel itself. We expect physics and math to be complex—why not the truth of God's revelation? So, instead of reducing the Gospel to soundbites we ought to grasp the whole counsel of God and wrestle with "the manifold wisdom of God" (Ephesians 3:10).

Faith does not operate in a different realm from sight. Faith is the earnest expectation of sight. In the most real world the two are inseparably linked and inherent in objective reality. "Without faith," wrote the author of Hebrews, "it is impossible to please him, for whoever would draw near to God must believe that he exists and that he rewards those who seek him" (Hebrews 11:6). Sight does not create that which is seen, nor does faith create that which is believed. If seeing meant believing for the first disciples, then believing means seeing for today's disciples. The resurrection of Christ is a fact of science and history that is believed by faith. If the resurrection of Christ did not actually happen in real time and real history, the apostle Paul spelled out the verdict: our faith is useless and we are guilty of bearing false witness. We are still in our sins and we are lost, without hope in the world. "If in this life only we have hoped in Christ, we are of all people most to be pitied" (1 Corinthians 15:19).

There is order, beauty, meaning, and joy woven into the very nature of creation. Everything points to a complexity that is neither random nor lucky. There is an inherent revelatory quality in all aspects of life. Creation is always beckoning for greater exploration, always inviting a deeper experience, always pointing beyond itself, and always bearing testimony not only to its many truths, but to the one and only singular truth. It is this truth that Jesus sums up when he says, "I am the way, the truth, and the life, no one comes to the Father but by me" (John 14:6). The empty tomb is a coherent testimony that the world is not the product of luck or magic. The world is called into existence by the will and word of God. "By faith we understand that the universe was created by the word of God, so that what is seen was not made out of things that are visible" (Hebrews 11:3).

THE NEW BIOLOGY

"Every living thing is an elaboration on a single original plan," writes Bill Bryson. "It cannot be said too often: all life is one. That is, and I suspect will forever prove to be, the most profound true statement there is."[2] The old biology is awed that human beings are so closely related to fruits and vegetables and that over 60 percent of human genes are the same as those in fruit flies. The scientific view of the human person is inevitably and understandably reductionistic, breaking down the person into component parts, reading DNA, mapping genomes, and discovering proteomes. This effort is true as far as it goes. The old biology aims to explain the *what, where, when,* and *how,* but it doesn't come close to explaining the *who.* Meaning has no casual connection to molecular structure, but there would be no molecular structure without it.

By contrast, the new biology is awed that human beings in Christ will be raised up in immortality. The new biology has set its sights on the future promise. The perishable will become imperishable. Death is not the final word after all. Redemption answers creation's longing. The old biology spirals downward into the amazing complexity of the so-called simple cell. The new biology spirals upward into the revelation of God's will and wisdom. The singularity of the original plan and the oneness of life originate in the word of God. "By faith we understand that the universe was formed at God's command, so that what is seen was not made out of what was visible" (Hebrews 11:3). All things are sustained moment by moment by this powerful word (Hebrews 1:3).

Issues of life and death highlight the absolute singularity of Christ. Jesus said, "I am the resurrection and the life. Anyone who believes in me will live, even though they die; and whoever lives by believing in me will never die" (John 11:25–26). The cross of Jesus and his atoning sacrifice targets the tragedy of sin and evil for redemption. "For the wages of sin is death, but the gift of God is eternal life in Christ Jesus our Lord" (Romans 6:23).

Our movies, art, literature, drama, poetry, and news media cover the horror of evil from virtually every angle, but provide little hope for redemption. The human story, even when it is told with pathos and creativity, continues to confirm that humanity cannot save itself. Everyone has a story but only one story redeems our story. The passion of Christ gathers up all of our sins and nature's evils—our idolatries, betrayals, addictions, deceptions, diseases, and hatreds and nails them to the cross. The tragedy of evil and God's redemptive love lead slowly and painstakingly to the cross—all for the sake of our salvation. The necessity of this cruciform culmination was woven into the events of salvation history from the beginning.

Likewise, the necessity of the resurrection of Jesus was woven into the very nature of creation. If history's need points to the cross, creation's mysteries point to the resurrection. The meaning of the resurrection cannot be packaged into a neat fool-proof apologetic, but it can be understood. We cannot explain it so as to control it or manipulate it, but we can marvel at its wisdom. We can grasp its meaning, comprehend its truth, but we cannot package it for easy consumption. From what we know of creation, the resurrection "makes sense." It fits. The resurrection was not some wild card, played at the end, which doesn't correspond with what we know of nature. The new biology fits in with the old biology. Like many things in science that we never would have expected to be true, the resurrection is consistent and coherent with what we know of reality. The same God who created the cosmos raised Christ from the dead. The more we know of this scientific world of ours, the greater the sheer wonder, astonishment and amazement at the power of the resurrection. Wonder is not antithetical to understanding. Given what we know, not what we don't know, the resurrection makes perfect sense and evokes the truest amazement.

IN HISTORY BUT NOT OF HISTORY

If the bones of Jesus disintegrated in a Palestinian tomb, then the fact and meaning of the Christian faith dissolve. If the Resurrection is reduced from historical fact to myth and metaphor, then the convergence we have been arguing for between creation and redemption, nature and grace, is canceled out. Since Jesus was "not abandoned to the grave, nor did his body see decay," the apostle Peter boldly affirmed, "God has made this Jesus, whom you crucified, both Lord and Christ" (Acts 2:31,36).

New Testament scholar Rudolf Bultmann claimed that a literal, physical resurrection was impossible. In his judgment, "an historical fact which involves a resurrection from the dead is utterly inconceivable!"[3] Bultmann denied the resurrection of Jesus insofar as it meant the return of a dead human being to life, but he affirmed Jesus' resurrection as an existential experience of freedom and self-understanding in the present life. For many professing believers who pride themselves on their sophistication, the resurrection stands for a positive outlook on life. They can't embrace it as the promised reality that assures them of an everlasting life with God. To them the resurrection is more believable as a desupernaturalized and dematerialized symbol for hope than the act of God that raised Jesus from the dead.

The Bible reasons that "there can be no purely historical explanation for the rise of the resurrection faith. It is due to an act of God which happened in history but did not happen in terms of historical causality."[4] How could it be otherwise? Hence the explanation for the reality of the Resurrection is found in God and believed by faith. But the Bible also asserts that resurrection faith is reasonable. It calls for an explanation. There is historical evidence for the wonder of the resurrection. The resurrection is a supernatural act without historical causality; nevertheless, it is a historical reality which helps explain the convictions and actions of the early Christians. There is an empirical, factual quality to the historical evidence for the resurrection.

If the resurrection didn't happen, there's some explaining to do. How do we account for the empty tomb, knowing that the authorities would have made every attempt possible to produce the body of Jesus in order to discredit the preaching of Jesus' resurrection? Is there an explanation for the radical change in the discouraged and bewildered disciples? Would these same men, who failed so miserably to stand with Jesus during his trial, go on to face persecution and death for the sake of a lie? Why do the biblical accounts of the resurrection draw significantly on the witness of women, when Jewish principles of evidence judged women as invalid witnesses? If the disciples were concerned only with a "symbolic" resurrection, why did they go out of their way to claim the historicity of Jesus resurrection? Why would they have documented his appearances and described their disbelief, if they wanted to say only that the spirit of Jesus' life survived his death and lived on in the proclamation of the gospel?

Christians have argued that the most reasonable answer to these questions is the reality of the bodily resurrection of Jesus. It has never been easy to believe in the Resurrection. The disciples had great difficulty coming to terms with this unexpected phenomenon. It was easier for them to believe that the body of Jesus had been stolen than to believe that Jesus had risen from the dead. There is no hint that the disciples were either intellectually or theologically prepared to believe in the resurrection of Jesus. It took them all by surprise. Contrary to their personal trauma, scriptural interpretation, and intellectual outlook, they came to believe in the reality of the resurrection. Something had to *happen* to make the *risen* Lord Jesus central to their powerful, dangerous preaching. Christians have believed that, in light of the whole history of Jesus, the most reasonable explanation for the empty tomb, the disciples' courage, and the biblical description of his appearances was in fact the resurrection of Jesus. Faith did not create the Resurrection; the Resurrection created faith.

Thomas' famous ultimatum was necessary. Of all the disciples, he was the one who refused to settle for anything less than empirical evidence. His insistence on a real resurrection was valid. "Unless I see the nail marks in his hands and put my finger where the nails were, and put my hand into his side, I will not believe it." He discounted what seemed to him to be strange and unfounded reports of Jesus' appearance first offered by women and then by the disciples behind locked doors. Thomas would have nothing to do with their wishful thinking. If he is going to believe in the Resurrection, it must be a real resurrection. If Jesus did not personally confront him with an actual body, he would reject any notion of resurrection. It is either a bodily resurrection or nothing at all. A modern writer, John Updike, expresses Thomas' feelings: *"Let us not mock God with metaphor, analogy, sidestepping transcendence; making of the event a parable, a sign painted in the faded credulity of earlier ages."*[5]

BEYOND NATURAL CAUSES

The apostle Paul agreed with Thomas' insistence on a real resurrection. Without the bodily resurrection of Jesus, the apostle Paul admitted that Christian preaching was useless, faith in Christ was futile, and the burden of sin remained. As far as Paul was concerned, Christianity without the Resurrection had no credibility. If God did not raise Jesus from the dead, believers were false witnesses of God, without hope, who ought to be "pitied more than all people" (1 Corinthians 15:14–19). Without the resurrection the gospel not only doesn't make sense, it is in fact, dishonest and deceptive. If there is no resurrection from the dead then death ends all and all are lost.

Biologists, astronomers, and physicists are familiar with the "inconceivable" becoming comprehensible. Much of what science knows to be true today about the cosmos and the cell was beyond imagining less than a hundred years ago. What we have learned about creation makes the resurrection credible. The universe itself has gone from a form we cannot understand to one we almost can. Cosmologists contemplate the process from nothingness to our space time universe. Why do we believe scientists when they say that the core of a neutron star is so dense that single spoonful of matter from it would weigh 200 billion pounds? We accept without fainting the astronomer's claim that there are 140 billion galaxies in the visible universe.[6] We believe in atoms, even though they measure one ten-millionth of a millimeter. That is to say that the width of one atom is to the width of a millimeter line as the thickness of a sheet of paper is to the height of the Empire State Building.[7] Geologists tell us that Yellowstone is a supervolcano, sitting on top of an enormous reservoir of molten rock forty-five miles across, and we believe them. Biologists marvel at the inner universe of the cell. "Of the twenty-three main divisions of life, only three—plants, animals, and fungi—are large enough to be seen by the human eye."[8] Microbes make up at least 80 percent of life on this planet. Your mattress is home to perhaps two million microscopic mites, but we were unaware of their intimate presence until 1965. We are all finding out that "life is infinitely more clever and adaptable than anyone had ever supposed."[9]

The validity of the bodily resurrection of Jesus rests in the sovereign will of God who is more than able to create an imperishable body, the nature of which is beyond anything we could imagine. Ultimately we believe that no natural explanation can account for either the first Adam or the second Adam. Humanly speaking we are no closer to believing in God our Creator than we are to believing in God our Savior. The truth of creation is no easier to accept than the truth about salvation. In both cases we are face to face with the mystery of God and His work. There is a logical connection between creation and redemption, natural life and supernatural life, but not a causal connection. In both cases we are dependent upon the revelation of God to bring home the truth of God and give us eyes to see and ears to hear what God has done for us and will do for us.

Paul's argument for the resurrection of the body draws on the science of nature.

> What you sow does not come to life unless it dies. When you sow, you do not plant the body that will be, but just a seed, perhaps of wheat or of something else. But God gives it a body as he has determined, and to each kind of seed he gives its own body. (1 Corinthians 15:36–38)

Paul saw a pattern in nature that helped him understand the resurrection of the body. A tiny seed is buried in the ground, it germinates, its outer shell dries out and cracks, and it begins to sprout. Slowly, the seed is transformed from a little, hard-shelled pebble into a flowering plant. If we didn't know better, it would be hard to imagine the relationship between an acorn and an oak tree or a zygote and a human person. Like a wise biologist or a good theologian, Paul gives God the credit for this amazing natural transformation and drives home the point that no one can imagine what the resurrected body will be like. The nature of this new body is completely up to God and beyond our ability to conceive.

Paul also observed the differences between species: "All flesh is not the same: Human beings have one kind of flesh, animals have another, birds another and fish another" (1 Corinthians 15:39).

Paul used the term "flesh" in a variety of ways; here he used it to indicate the external, physical differences between humans, animals, birds and fish. Today's scientific emphasis is usually on the relatedness of all living organisms, but it only takes a trip to the San Diego Zoo or Petco Park, where the San Diego Padres play, to be reminded of the amazing diversity of life. Instead of dwelling on the cell structure or the molecular nature of organisms, which he knew nothing about, Paul marveled at the seemingly infinite variety of living organisms, a truth no sensible person would deny. In the phenomenal diversity of life, Paul found logical support for the reality of the resurrected body. It was conceivable that the God of such a wonderfully diverse creation was fully capable of doing as he promised and creating a new, glorified, resurrected body.

Paul's observations move out from the tiny seed to the immensity of space.

> There are also heavenly bodies and there are earthly bodies, but the splendor of the heavenly bodies is one kind, and the

splendor of the earthly bodies is another. The sun has one kind
of splendor, the moon another and the stars another; and star
differs from star in splendor. (1 Corinthians 15:40–41)

The planets and stars have their own unique splendor which
set them apart from one another. They may share common
elements but they are studied and appreciated for their unique-
ness. Wherever Paul looked he saw this amazing diversity in
creation bolstering his confidence in the reality of the resurrection. Nature's pattern of incredible transformation, phenomenal diversity, and amazing splendor, made faith in the resurrection credible for Paul. Based on God's promise and these
illustrations from nature, Paul concluded that it was reasonable
to believe in the resurrection of the body.

However, the conclusions he drew from creation did not
imply any natural continuity or naturalistic explanation for
the resurrection. There was nothing in nature itself that led to
this new creation. Just the opposite was true. Paul stressed the
difference between the perishable body and the imperishable
body. He stressed the discontinuity between the natural body
and the spiritual body. The old creation, with its tremendous
diversity of "bodies" illustrates the creative power of God but
offers no clue as to the nature of the resurrection. The connection between the old creation and the new creation is neither
natural nor physical, but relational. The link between them
is in the mind of God, but make no mistake, they are two
separate works. The reality of the natural realm does not exist
as a platonic shadow or as a scientific prototype of the world to
come, but as a testimony of the power and wisdom of God.

"So will it be with the resurrection of the dead. The body that
is sown is perishable, it is raised imperishable; it is sown in
dishonor, it is raised in glory; it is sown in weakness, it is raised

in power; it is sown a natural body, it is raised a spiritual body."
(1 Corinthians 15:42–44)

Paul's description of the difference between these two "bodies" captures the pathos of the human condition and the expectation of the new creation. The contrast is not between bodily decay and a bodiless existence, but between a natural life of death and a spiritual life of living. On this side of eternity, bodily death is part and parcel of biological living. It factors in everywhere from reproduction to digestion to circulation. Apart from death, we would be unable to live. But in the new creation, bodily existence will be characterized by life, not death. Now life is characterized by death and dying, grief and humiliation, frailty and weakness, but a new day is coming, when the key to life will not be death but life. The inevitability of decay, shame, and weakness will be eliminated by the life, glory, and power of the resurrection. And this new, glorified, resurrected body will surpass the limitations of a natural body. It will embrace the fullness of personal identity and experience the richness of community life. This risen body will include the whole person and will be nothing like the Greek notion of a bodyless, immortal soul or the modern idea of the spirit of a person living on in people's memory. The spiritual body is no less real than the natural body, though, at this point, we can't imagine what our spiritual bodies will be like.

The fact that there are two types of bodily existence helps us put the struggle of human existence in perspective. If we have only this body to contend with, then cosmetic surgery and spare-no-expense pleasure seeking are eminently reasonable endeavors. The full-court medical press to extend life and forestall death also makes a lot of sense, as do elaborate funerals with expensive coffins and memorial headstones. If bodily existence is limited to the physical then we ought to be thorough-going materialists. But the natural life, rooted as it is in death, is only part of the story. "If there is a natural body," Paul reasoned, "there is also a spiritual body." For Paul this was not a huge leap, as it might be for some today, because he was convinced that the God of creation was also the God of redemption. Not only was humanity made in the image of God, but God became human, in order to redeem humanity from sin and death. The resurrection of Jesus is the "firstfruits" of a whole new harvest; it is the key that unlocks the door to a whole new order. There are no humanistic resources that can transform the natural life into the spiritual life and triumph over death. "I declare to you, brothers and sisters, that flesh and blood cannot inherit the kingdom of God, nor does the perishable inherit the imperishable" (1 Corinthians 15:50).

Paul further understood the contrast between death-defining natural life and death-defying spiritual life by turning to salvation history. If the wonderful diversity of creation points to the power of God to create an entirely new mode of existence, then the message of salvation history declares that there is much more to life than the old Adam. The first Adam stands for sin and death; he represents the fallen human condition. The last Adam stands for salvation and life; he represents the "first-fruits" of the new creation. It doesn't take a genius to conclude that "the first Adam was of the dust of the earth," but it is tragic that some of our best minds stop there! Why do intellectuals become famous for observing a half-truth—and an illogical half-truth at that? If men and women are ultimately only dust, mere accidental freaks of nature, why does it take so much human ingenuity to make the case? The wisdom of this age believes in the first Adam's dust but not in the last Adam's life. But the apostle Paul linked the two together in the saving work of God. In the light of the revelation of God, it is illogical to insist on a half-truth at the expense of God's saving truth in Christ. Paul is able to move from dust to destiny, and from death to life, because of the last Adam, a life-giving spirit. "And just as we have borne the likeness of the earthly man," Paul insisted, "so shall we bear the likeness of the heavenly man" (1 Corinthians 15:49).

Paul drew his spiritual direction to a close by reaffirming that it is only the power of the Cross that can free us from sin and death. Only God can transform the natural life into the spiritual life and triumph over death. Paul's summation is not a rhetorical flourish, but an earnest plea for the believers to come to their senses and put their trust in God. Having demonstrated the logic of the resurrection on the basis of God's work in creation and redemption, and having insisted that whatever is dying cannot achieve life, Paul brings his argument to a climax by emphasizing the final consummation. Neither creation nor history are best understood as an endless cycle of reoccurring patterns nor a linear stream of events with no conclusion. Neither creation nor history are ruled by fate. Both are ruled by the sovereign Lord, and the ultimate transformation for which we yearn will not happen until God's appointed end.

The ultimate transformation we need and long for cannot be achieved gradually through any natural, "flesh and blood" means, but only through the work of God creating for us a new, glorified, resurrected body. When Paul says, "I tell you a mystery," he means "mystery." He is not offering a puzzle to test our ingenuity, nor a problem that requires speculation, but a promise that calls for trust because it is completely beyond our calculations, much less our control.

There is no hidden knowledge waiting to be discovered by a self-styled spiritual elite who pride themselves on being in the know. The mystery lies in the nature and timing of a transformation that belongs absolutely to the Lord. We do not know how the perishable will clothe itself with the imperishable, nor do we have any idea how mortals will put on immortality. But by faith we believe "the dead will be raised imperishable, and we will be changed." For it is only then that Isaiah's prophecy will come true, "Death has been swallowed up in victory" (see Isaiah 25:8).

The imagery of death being swallowed up in victory is worth contemplating. The very idea that death itself, the undeniable fact of life that looms larger than any other fear, will be consumed in a bite and a gulp is so radical that it defies humanistic explanation. We react to the immensity and the inevitability of death with defiance and denial, contempt and fear. We throw everything we have in science and philosophy against death, but nothing brings it down to size. We may delay it, but we cannot stop it. We may numb its pain, but we cannot shrink its tragedy. All of our death-defying tactics are destined for defeat against an enemy so overwhelming that nothing can overcome it. Nothing, that is, but the risen Lord, who has the power to reduce the monster to a miserable morsel. That which threatens to engulf us is swallowed up. Praise God! "Death has been swallowed up in victory."

Emboldened by this truth, Paul talks back to death. It is not as if he is shaking his fist at death. It is more like he is standing over a defeated enemy. He draws on the prophet Hosea's personification of death in order to deliver his mocking taunt, "Where, O death, is your victory? Where, O death, is your sting?" (1 Corinthians 15:55; see Hosea 13:14). Death has been rendered powerless, poisonless. It no longer has the ultimate power to destroy us. Death is stingless because Christ absorbed the venom for us. On the Cross he took upon himself the consequences of our sin and evil. "The sting of death is sin, and the power of sin is the law." Paul has been careful to leave the climactic truth for the end. "But thanks be to God! He gives us the victory through our Lord Jesus Christ" (1 Corinthians 15:57).

INESCAPABLE WONDER

To my surprise, "luck" is a major concept pulled in by modern writers to make sense of life. "Luck" never shows up in their indexes, but it is offered as a major explanation for the origin of life and hope for the future. Richard Dawkins attributes both the origin of life and the origin of human consciousness to luck. Two big ones if you ask me! "Once that initial stroke of luck has been granted," argues Dawkins, we're off and running with evolution.[10]

Bill Bryson concludes his masterful work on the science of life by saying how "awfully lucky" we are to be here—"doubly lucky" in fact, because we have the singular ability to appreciate the privilege of existence. He credits our survival to "a nearly endless string of good fortune." We are only at the beginning of this "one planet, one experiment" experience, but we will "require a good deal more than lucky breaks" to "make sure we never find the end."[11]

If luck is the best explanation for the origin of life and hope for the future; if love is little more than a biological drive to pass along our genes; if meaning is entirely self-created; then wonder is best described as a strange mood that comes over us at odd times. Meaning and wisdom are only illusions. In an uncreated world of nature alone, joy is an individual stroke of good luck. Present moment happiness is the key. Nobel laureate Francis Crick summed us up this way: "*You*, your joys and your sorrows, your memories and your ambitions, your sense of personal identity and free will, are in fact no more than the behavior of a vast assembly of nerve cells and their associated molecules."[12]

The thorough-going materialist handles death very differently than the apostle Paul. The materialist need neither defy nor fear death, because death is nothing at all. Before becoming a Christian, C.S. Lewis was comforted by the thought that death ended all. "The materialist's universe had the enormous attraction that . . . death ended all . . . And if ever finite disasters proved greater than one wished to bear, suicide would always be possible. The horror of the Christian universe was that it had no door marked *Exit*."[13] For the materialist, the last thing to reduce to nothing is death. For the Christian, the last thing to triumph over is death. The empty tomb means that life has been emptied of nothingness and filled with meaning.

I mentioned earlier the wonder of holding my newborn daughter and feeling the glory of God. What is even more strange and wonderful is the experience of the glory of God at the bedside of a dying loved one. How in the presence of death is it possible for us to have a palpable sense that death does not end all? It is this unexpected surprise, not of a wishful dream, but of resurrection hope that lays hold not only of the heart but the mind. The "incomprehensible" becomes comprehensible. Ultimately the power of the explanation shifts. It is not we who explain the resurrection but the resurrection that explains us. We are not in control of the truth, the truth is in control of us.

"If the dead are not raised," Paul contends, then "Let us eat and drink, for tomorrow we die." If there is no resurrection, or if the resurrection is only believed on in a pious, symbolic way, then there is no reason to live for anything else but the self. There is nothing else to seek than present-moment happiness and nothing else to be gained but personal pleasure. If there is no resurrection then a self-indulgent, me-first lifestyle is the way to go.

If, through the power of the Holy Spirit, we believe by faith in the resurrection of Christ, we will not think of Jesus as an inspirational memory but as the living Lord. Instead of funeral services that offer a generic "celebration of life," our memorial services will witness to the power and hope of the risen Lord Jesus. Our investment strategy and giving will be guided by the hope of everlasting life rather than the anticipation of a long retirement. We will not think of Jesus as the founder of a religious tradition, but as the coming King who will rule and reign forever and ever. Like the apostle Paul, we will be willing to risk our careers, our resources, our reputations, even our lives, because of our hope of the resurrection.

Resurrection faith does not call for a sacrifice of the believer's intellect. However, unless there is a personal encounter with the risen Lord, eliciting the exclamation of worship, "My Lord and my God," the evidence ultimately matters little. Unquestionably Thomas' situation was unique. He actually saw the body of Jesus. Consequently the requirement of faith becomes the greater for those who follow after Thomas. As Jesus said, "Blessed are those who have not seen and yet have believed" (John 20:29).

*Oh, the depth of the riches of the
wisdom and knowledge of God!*

*How unsearchable his judgments, and
his paths beyond tracing out!*

*Who has known the mind of the Lord?
Or who has been his counselor?*

*Who has ever given to God, that
God should repay them?*

*For from him and through him
and to him are all things.*

To him be the glory forever! Amen.

Romans 11:33–36

NOTES

Chapter 1: Meaningless! Meaningless!

1. Benjamin Wiker and Jonathan Witt, *A Meaningful World: How the Arts and Sciences Reveal the Genius of Nature* (Downers Grove, IL: InterVarsity, 2006), 16.
2. Steven Weinberg, *The First Three Minutes: A Modern View of the Origin of the Universe* (New York: Basic Books, 1977), 154–55.
3. Wiker and Witt, *Meaningful World*, 24.

Chapter 2: Mere Mortals

1. Armand M. Nicholi Jr., *The Question of God: C. S. Lewis and Sigmund Freud Debate God, Love, Sex, and the Meaning of Life* (New York: Free Press, 2002), 6.
2. Derek Kidner, *Psalms 1–72: An Introduction and Commentary* (Downers Grove, IL: InterVarsity, 1973), 65–66.
3. Mark Steyn, *America Alone: The End of the World as We Know It* (Washington, DC: Regnery, 2006), 4.
4. Richard Dawkins, *The God Delusion* (Boston: Houghton Mifflin, 2006), 172.
5. C. S. Lewis, *Surprised by Joy* (London: Fontana, 1972), 170.
6. Ibid., 177.
7. Ibid., 181.
8. Ibid., 182.
9. John Stott, *Christian Mission in the Modern World* (Downers Grove, IL: InterVarsity, 1975), 29–30.

10. Daniel Defoe, *Robinson Crusoe* (New York: Random House, 1988), 97.

11. Ibid., 102.

12. Ibid., 106.

13. Ibid., 126.

14. Carl F. H. Henry, *God, Revelation, and Authority* (Waco, TX: Word, 1976), 1:225.

15. Francis Crick, *The Astonishing Hypothesis: The Scientific Search for the Soul* (New York: Simon and Schuster, 1994), 3, 256–57, 260.

16. R. Buckminster Fuller, quoted in Lewis Mumford, *The Myth of the Machine* (New York: Harcourt Brace and World, 1970), 56.

17. Loren Eiseley, "The Cosmic Orphan," *Encyclopedia Britannica*, 1974.

18. Alexander Pope, *Essay on Man* (Mineola, NY: Dover, 1994), 19.

19. Carl Sagan, *A Pale Blue Dot* (New York: Random House, 1994), 405.

20. Blaise Pascal, *Pensées* (New York: Penguin, 1966), 55.

21. John Calvin, *Institutes of the Christian Religion*, trans. Henry Beveridge (Grand Rapids: Eerdmans, 1981), 1:37.

22. Kidner, *Psalms 1–72*, 67.

23. William Shakespeare, *Hamlet* (New York: Dorset, 1988), 2.11.

24. Pascal, *Pensées*, 170.

25. C. S. Lewis, *The Weight of Glory* (New York: Collier, 1980), 7

Chapter 3: The Ultimate Knower

1. Lewis, *Surprised by Joy*, 176.

2. Sigmund Freud, *The Future of an Illusion* (New York: W. W. Norton, 1989), 24.

3. Dawkins, *God Delusion*, 147.

4. Richard Dawkins, "The Evolution Wars," *Time*, August 15, 2005, 32.

5. Ibid.

6. Dawkins, *God Delusion*, 117.

7. Ibid., 117

8. Timothy Johnson, *Finding God in the Questions* (Downers Grove, IL: InterVarsity, 2004), 33.

9. Bill Bryson, *A Short History of Nearly Everything* (New York: Broadway, 2004), 145.

10. Ibid., 219.

11. Dawkins, "The Evolution Wars," 34.

12. Dawkins, *God Delusion*, 117.

13. Duane Litfin, *Conceiving the Christian College* (Grand Rapids: Eerdmans, 2004), 190.

14. Richard Dawkins, *River Out of Eden* (New York: Basic Books, 1995), 95.

15. Francis S. Collins, *The Language of God* (New York: Free Press, 2006), 29.

16. Ibid., 22.

17. Ibid., 28, 30.

18. Randall Smith, "The Love That Moves the Sun," *The Creative Spirit* 4, no. 3 (2006–2007), 55.

Chapter 4: The Language of God

1. Johnson, *Finding God in the Questions*, 56; Dawkins, *God Delusion*, 104.

2. Richard Baxter, *The Reformed Pastor* (Carlisle, PA: Banner of Truth, 2007), 56–57.

3. Parker J. Palmer, *The Courage to Teach: Exploring the Inner Landscape of a Teacher's Life* (San Francisco: Jossey-Bass, 1998), 110.

4. Philip E. Johnson, "The Wedge in Evolutionary Ideology: Its History, Strategy, and Agenda," *Theology Matters* (March/April 1999), 5.

5. Quoted in William Dembski, "Admitting Design into Science," *Theology Matters* (March/April 1999), 8.

6. Eugene H. Peterson, "Novelists, Pastors, Poets," *Crux* 26, no. 4 (1990), 3.

7. Collins, *Language of God*, 2–3, 119.

8. Ibid., 125.

9. Barry Commoner, "Unraveling the DNA Myth: The Spurious Foundation of Genetic Engineering," *Harper's* (February 2002), 39–47.

10. Ibid.

11. Collins, *Language of God*, 125.

12. Commoner, "Unraveling the DNA Myth," 39–47.

13. Bryson, *Short History of Nearly Everything*, 410.

14. Ibid., 408.

15. Ibid., 399.

16. Ibid., 408.

17. Commoner, "Unraveling the DNA Myth," 39–47.

18. Lewis, *Mere Christianity*, 25.

19. Quoted in Wiker and Witt, *A Meaningful World*, 100.

20. Ibid., 101.

21. Thomas Dubay, *The Evidential Power of Beauty* (San Francisco: Ignatius, 1999), 346.

22. Eugene H. Peterson, *Reversed Thunder: The Revelation of John and the Praying Imagination* (San Francisco: Harper & Row, 1988), 16.
23. Dubay, *The Evidential Power of Beauty*, 57.
24. Ibid., 58.
25. Ibid., 58.
26. Wiker and Witt, *A Meaningful World*, 190.
27. Dawkins, *God Delusion*, 87.
28. Ibid., 86–87.
29. Quoted in Rory Noland, *The Heart of the Artist* (Grand Rapids: Zondervan, 1999), 27.
30. Lewis, *The Weight of Glory*, 7.
31. Kidner, *Psalms 1–72*, 99.
32. Peter C. Craigie, *Psalms 1–50* (Waco, TX: Word, 1983), 183.

Chapter 5: The Search for Meaning

1. Hugh Ross, *The Creator and the Cosmos* (Colorado Springs: NavPress, 1993), 111.
2. Dawkins, *God Delusion*, 136.
3. Ibid., 137.
4. Ibid., 138.
5. Ibid., 139–40.
6. Francis I. Anderson, *Job* (Downers Grove, IL: InterVarsity, 1976), 225.
7. Ibid., 224–25.
8. Bryson, *Short History of Nearly Everything*, 210.
9. Ibid., 218–19.
10. Lewis Thomas, *The Youngest Science* (New York: Penguin, 1995).
11. Lewis, *Miracles,* 46.
12. Wendell Berry, *Life Is a Miracle: An Essay Against Modern Superstition* (Washington, DC: Counterpoint, 2000), 7, 10.
13. Ibid., 19.
14. Ibid., 35.
15. G. K. Chesterton, *Orthodoxy* (New York: Image, 1959), 20, 23.
16. Franklin Harold, *The Way of the Cell: Molecules, Organisms, and the Order of Life* (Oxford: Oxford University Press, 2001), 66.
17. Lewis, *Mere Christianity*, 40–42.
18. Anderson, *Job*, 224.
19. Ibid., 268–69.
20. Ibid., 287.
21. Søren Kierkegaard, *Training in Christianity* (Princeton: Princeton University Press, 1957), 131.

22. Lewis, *Mere Christianity*, 165.

Chapter 6: All Things Hold Together

1. Dubay, *The Evidential Power of Beauty*, 328.

2. Nancy Pearcey, *Total Truth: Liberating Christianity from Its Cultural Captivity* (Wheaton, IL: Crossway, 2005), 19.

3. Tim Stafford, "Favorite-Song Theology," *Christianity Today*, September 14, 1992, 36–38.

4. Harry Blamires, *The Christian Mind* (London: SPCK, 1978), 119–20.

5. Dubay, *The Evidential Power of Beauty*, 40.

6. Quoted in Dawkins, *God Delusion*, 15.

7. Karl Barth, *Dogmatics in Outline* (New York: Harper & Row, 1959), 50, 52.

8. Bryson, *Short History of Nearly Everything*, 27.

9. Lewis, *Miracles*, 121.

10. Ibid., 122.

11. Ibid., 122.

12. Dante, *Paradisio*, ed. Mark Musa (New York: Penguin, 1995), 33.67–93.

13. Blamires, *The Christian Mind*, 173.

14. Lewis, *Mere Christianity*, 60, 63–64.

15. Søren Kierkegaard, *Purity of Heart Is to Will One Thing* (New York: Harper & Row, 1956), 138.

Chapter 7: The Empty Tomb and the New Biology

1. Weinberg, *First Three Minutes*, 154.

2. Bryson, *Short History of Nearly Everything*, 415.

3. Rudolf Bultmann, *Kerygma and Myth*, ed. Hans Werner Bartsch (New York: Harper & Row, 1961), 39.

4. I. Howard Marshall, *Luke: Historian and Theologian* (Grand Rapids: Zondervan, 1982), 48.

5. Richard Lischer, "'Resurrexit': Something to Preach," *Christian Century*, April 2, 1980, 372, quoting John Updike, *Telephone Poles and Other Poems* (New York: Knopf, 1963).

6. Bryson, *Short History of Nearly Everything*, 32, 129.

7. Ibid., 135.

8. Ibid., 311.

9. Ibid., 235, 365.

10. Dawkins, *God Delusion*, 140–41.

11. Bryson, *Short History of Nearly Everything*, 478.
12. Crick, *Astonishing Hypothesis*, 3.
13. Lewis, *Surprised by Joy*, 139.

LaVergne, TN USA
04 April 2011
222822LV00004B/24/P